VOLVO PENTA MD2010, MD2020, MD2030, MD2040

Workshop Manual

VOLVO PENTA MD2010, MD2020, MD2030, MD2040

Workshop Manual

ISBN/EAN: 9783954275069
Erscheinungsjahr: 2012
Erscheinungsort: Bremen, Deutschland

© maritimepress in Europäischer Hochschulverlag GmbH & Co. KG, Fahrenheitstr. 1, 28359 Bremen. Alle Rechte beim Verlag und bei den jeweiligen Lizenzgebern.

www.maritimepress.de | office@maritimepress.de

Bei diesem Titel handelt es sich um den Nachdruck eines historischen, lange vergriffenen Buches. Da elektronische Druckvorlagen für diese Titel nicht existieren, musste auf alte Vorlagen zurückgegriffen werden. Hieraus zwangsläufig resultierende Qualitätsverluste bitten wir zu entschuldigen.

VOLVO PENTA MD2010, MD2020, MD2030, MD2040

Workshop Manual

Workshop Manual

Marine engines

MD2010A/B/C · MD2020A/B/C · MD2030A/B/C · MD2040A/B/C

Contents

Technical data

Injection pump	9
Wear tolerances	15
Tightening torque	17

Special tools

	18

Presentation

Description of engine	19

Engine body

Description	24
Repair instructions:	
Cylinder head	25
Valves, valve mechanism	28
Cylinder block, pistons, connecting rods	34
Timing gears	40
Camshaft	44
Crank mechanism	46

Lubricating system

Description	51
Repair instructions	
Oil pump	52
Replacing the oil filter	52
Cleaning the oil channels	52

Fuel system

Description	53

Repair instructions

Injection pump	54
Adjustment of injection angle	55
Adjustment of speed	57
Feed pump	58
Fuel filter	59
Bleeding of fuel system	59
Injector	60
Checking of injector	61

Cooling system

Description	62
Repair instructions	
Refrigerants	63
Checking of refrigerant level	64
Cleaning	65
Circulation pump	66
Sea water pump	66
Replacing the thermostat	67
Checking the thermostat	67

Electrical system

Description	68
Important info	70
Starting with auxiliary battery	71
Troubleshooting, glow plug, charging system	72
Alternator	74
Starter motor	76
Electrical components	78
Wiring diagram	80
Extra equipment	87

Note!

The data given in this Workshop Manual refers in general to engines in both A, B and C versions unless otherwise stated.

Safety Precautions

Introduction

This Workshop Manual contains technical specifications, descriptions and instructions for the repair of the Volvo Penta products or product types described in the Table of Contents. Check that you have the correct Workshop Manual for your engine.

Before starting work on the engine read the "Safety Precautions", "General Information" and "Repair Instruction" sections of this Workshop Manual carefully.

Important

In this book and on the product you will find the following special warning symbols.

 WARNING! Possible danger of personal injury, extensive damage to property or serious mechanical malfunction if the instructions are not followed.

 IMPORTANT! Used to draw your attention to something that can cause damage or malfunctions on a product or damage to property.

Note! Used to draw your attention to important information that will facilitate the work or operation in progress.

Below is a summary of the risks involved and safety precautions you should always observe or carry out when operating or servicing the engine.

Immobilize the engine by turning off the power supply to the engine at the main switch (switches) and lock it (them) in the OFF position before starting work. Set up a warning notice at the engine control point or helm.

As a general rule all service operations must be carried out with the engine stopped. However, some work, for example certain adjustments require that the engine is running when they are carried out. Approaching an engine which is operating is a safety risk. Loose clothing or long hair can fasten in rotating parts and cause serious personal injury. If working in proximity of an engine which is operating, careless movements or a dropped tool can result in personal injury. Take care to avoid contact with hot surfaces (exhaust pipes, Turbocharger (TC), air intake pipe, start element etc.) and hot liquids in lines and hoses on an engine which is running or which has just been stopped. Reinstall all protective parts removed during service operations before starting the engine.

Check that the warning or information labels on the product are always clearly visible. Replace labels which have been damaged or painted over.

Engines with turbocharger (TC): Never start the engine without installing the air cleaner (ACL) filter. The rotating compressor in the Turbo can cause serious personal injury. Foreign objects entering the intake ducts can also cause mechanical damage.

Never use start spray products or similar when starting the engine. They may cause an explosion in the inlet manifold. Danger of personal injury.

 Avoid opening the filler cap for engine coolant system (freshwater cooled engines) when the engine is still hot. Steam or hot coolant can spray out. Open the filler cap slowly and release the pressure in the system. Take great care if a cock, plug or engine coolant line must be removed from a hot engine. Steam or hot coolant can spray out in any direction.

Hot oil can cause burns. Avoid getting hot oil on the skin. Ensure that the lubrication system is not under pressure before carrying out any work. Never start or operate the engine with the oil filler cap removed, otherwise oil could be ejected.

Stop the engine and close the sea cock before carrying out operations on the engine cooling system.

Only start the engine in a well-ventilated area. If operating the engine in an enclosed area ensure that there is exhaust ventilation leading out of the engine compartment or workshop area to remove exhaust gases and crankcase ventilation emissions.

Always use protective glasses or goggles when carrying out work where there is a risk of splinters, grinding sparks, acid splashes or where other chemicals are used. The eyes are extremely sensitive, an injury could result in blindness!

O Avoid getting oil on the skin! Repeated exposure to oil or exposure over a long period can result in the skin becoming dry. Irritation, dryness and eczema and other skin problems can then occur. Used oil is more dangerous than fresh oil from a health aspect. Use protective gloves and avoid oil soaked clothes and shop rags. Wash regularly, especially before eating. There are special skin creams which counteract drying out of the skin and make it easier to clean off dirt after work is completed.

Many chemicals used on the product (for example engine and transmission oils, glycol, gasoline and diesel oil), or chemicals used in the workshop (for example degreasing agents, paint and solvents) are dangerous to health. Read the instructions on the product packaging carefully! Always follow the safety precautions for the product (for example use of protective mask, glasses, gloves etc.). Make sure that other personnel are not exposed to hazardous chemicals, for example in the air. Ensure good ventilation in the work place. Follow the instructions provided when disposing of used or leftover chemicals.

IL Excercise extreme care when leak detecting on the fuel system and testing the fuel injector jets. Use eye protection. The jet from a fuel injector nozzle is under extremely high pressure and has great penetrative energy, so the fuel can penetrate deep into the body tissue and cause serious personal injury. Danger of blood poisoning.

O All fuels and many chemical substances are flammable. Do not allow naked flame or sparks in the vicinity. Fuel, certain thinner products and hydrogen from batteries can be extremely flammable and explosive when mixed with air. Smoking is not to be permitted in the vicinity! Ensure that the work area is well ventilated and take the necessary safety precautions before starting welding or grinding work. Always ensure that there are fire extinguishers at hand when work is being carried out.

O Ensure that rags soaked in oil or fuel and used fuel or oil filters are stored safely. Rags soaked in oil can spontaneously ignite under certain circumstances. Used fuel and oil filters are environmentally dangerous waste and must be deposited at an approved site for destruction together with used lubricating oil, contaminated fuel, paint remnants, solvent, degreasing agents and waste from washing parts.

Never expose a battery to naked flame or electrical sparks. Never smoke in proximity to the batteries. The batteries give off hydrogen gas during charging which when mixed with air can form an explosive gas - oxyhydrogen. This gas is easily ignited and highly volatile. Incorrect connection of the battery can cause a single spark which is sufficient to cause an explosion with resulting damage. Do not shift the connections when attempting to start the engine (spark risk) and do not lean over any of the batteries.

2L Always ensure that the Plus (positive) and Minus (negative) battery leads are correctly installed on the corresponding terminal posts on the batteries. Incorrect installation can result in serious damage to the electrical equipment. Refer to the wiring diagrams.

O Always use protective goggles when charging and handling the batteries. Battery electrolyte contains sulfuric acid which is highly corrosive. Should the battery electrolyte come into contact with unprotected skin wash off immediately using plenty of water and soap. If battery acid comes in contact with the eyes, immediately flush with plenty of water and obtain medical assistance at once.

A Turn the engine off and turn off the power at the main switch(es) before carrying out work on the electrical system.

Clutch adjustments must be carried out with the engine stopped.

General Information

About this Workshop Manual

This Workshop Manual contains technical specifications, descriptions and instructions for the repair of the following engines in standard format: MD2010, MD2020, MD2030, MD2040. This Workshop Manual can show operations carried out on any of the engines listed above. As a result the illustrations and pictures in the manual that show certain parts on the engines, do not in some cases apply to all the engines listed. However the repair and service operations described are in all essential details the same. Where they are not the same this is stated in the manual and where the difference is considerable the operations are described separately. The Engine Designations and Engine Number can be found on the product plate. Please always include both the engine designation and the engine number in all correspondance.

The Workshop Manual is produced primarily for the use of Volvo Penta workshops and service technicians. For this reason the manual presupposes a certain basic knowledge of marine propulsion systems and that the user can carry out the mechanical/electrical work described to a general standard of engineering competence.

Volvo Penta products are under a continual process of development and we therefore reserve all rights regarding changes and modifications. All the information in this manual is based on product specifications available at the time the book was published. Any essential changes or modifications introduced into production or updated or revised service methods introduced after the date of publication will be provided in the form of Service Bulletins.

Replacement parts

Replacement parts for the electrical and fuel systems are subject to various national safety requirements, for example the United States Coast Guard Safety Regulations. Volvo Penta Original Spare Parts meet these specifications. Any type of damage which is the result of using replacement parts that are not original Volvo Penta replacement parts for the product in question will not be covered under any warranty or guarantee provided by AB Volvo Penta.

Certified engines

For engines certified for national and regional environmental legislation the manufacturer undertakes to ensure compliance with such environmental requirements for both new engines and engines is use. The product must comply with the approved example on certification. For Volvo Penta as the manufacturer to be able accept responsibility for the compliance of engines in use with the set environmental requirements, the following requirements for service and spare parts must be fulfilled:

- The service intervals and maintenance procedures recommended by Volvo Penta must be followed.

- Only Volvo Penta Genuine Spare Parts intended for the certified engine version must be used.

- Service of injection pumps, pump settings, and injectors, shall always be conducted by an authorised Volvo Penta workshop.

- The engine must not be rebuilt or modified in any way, with the exception of the accessories and service kits that Volvo Penta has developed for the engine.

- Installation adjustments on exhaust pipes and supply air channels for the engine compartment (ventilation channels) must not, without due care, be conducted since this can influence exhaust emissions.

- Seals must not be broken by unauthorised personnel.

IMPORTANT! Use only Volvo Penta Genuine Spare Parts. **The use of non genuine parts implies that AB Volvo Penta will no longer assume responsibility for compliance of the engine with the certified versions.** All types of damage or costs resulting from the use of non genuine Volvo Penta spare parts for the product in question will not be regulated by Volvo Penta.

Repair instructions and methods

The working methods described in the Workshop Manual apply to work carried out in a workshop. The engine has been removed from the boat and is installed in an engine fixture. Unless otherwise stated reconditioning work which can be carried out with the engine in place follows the same working method.

Warning symbols used in this Workshop Manual (for full explanation of the symbols refer to the section; "Safety Precautions")

⚠ **WARNING!**

⚠ **IMPORTANT!**

Note!

are not in any way comprehensive since it is impossible to predict every circumstance under which service work or repairs may be carried out. Volvo Penta AB can only indicate the risks considered likely to occur as a result of incorrect working methods in a well-equipped workshop using working methods and tools tested by Volvo Penta AB.

All operations described in the Workshop Manual for which there are Volvo Penta Special Tools available assume that these tools are used by the service technician or person carrying out the repair. Volvo Penta Special Tools have been specifically developed to ensure as safe and rational working methods as possible. It is therefore the responsibility of the person or persons using other than Volvo Penta Special Tools or approved Volvo Penta working methods (as described in a Workshop Manual or Service Bulletin), to acquaint themselves of the risk of personal injury or actual mechanical damage or malfunction that can result from failing to use the prescribed tools or working method.

In some cases special safety precautions and user instructions may be required in order to use the tools and chemicals mentioned in the Workshop Manual. Always follow these precautions as there are no specific instructions given in the Workshop Manual.

By following these basic recommendations and using common sense it is possible to avoid most of the risks involved in the work. A clean work place and a clean engine will eliminate many risks of personal injury and engine malfunction.

Above all when working on the fuel system, engine lubrication system, air intake system, Turbocharger unit, bearing seals and seals it is extremely important to observe the highest standards of cleanliness and avoid dirt or foreign objects entering the parts or systems, since this can result in reduced service life or malfunctions.

Our joint responsibility

Every engine consists of many systems and components that work together. If one component deviates from the technical specifications this can have dramatic consequences on the environmental impact of the engine even if it is otherwise in good running order. It is therefore critical that the stated wear tolerances are observed, that systems which can be adjusted are correctly set up and that only Volvo Penta Original Parts are used on the engine. The stated service intervals in the Maintenance Schedule must be followed.

Some systems, such as the components in the fuel system, require special expertise and special testing equipment for service and maintenance. Some components are factory sealed for environmental and product specific reasons. Under no circumstances attempt to service or repair a sealed component unless the service technician carrying out the work is authorized to do so.

Bear in mind that most of the chemicals used around boats are harmful to the environment if used incorrectly. Volvo Penta recommends the use of bio-degradable degreasing agents for all cleaning of engine components unless otherwise stated in the Workshop Manual. When working onboard a boat make a special point of preventing oil, waste water from washing components entering the bilges; instead remove all such waste for safe disposal at an approved site for destruction.

Tightening torques

The correct tightening torques for critical joints which must be tightened using a torque wrench are listed under "Technical Specifications - Tightening Torques" and stated in the method descriptions in the Workshop Manual. All tightening torques apply to cleaned threads, bolt heads and mating surfaces. Tigthening torques stated are for lightly oiled or dry threads. Where grease, locking or sealing agents are required for screwed joints this is stated in both the operation description and in "Tightening Torques". Where no tightening torque is stated for a joint use the general tightening torques according to the tables below. The tightening torques stated are a guide and the joint does not have to be tightened using a torque wrench.

Dimension	Tightening torque	
	Nm	ft.lbs
M5	6	4
M6	10	7
M8	25	18
M10	50	37
M12	80	59
M14	140	103

Tightening torque with Protractor tightening (angle tightening)

Tightening using both a torque setting and a protractor angle requires that first the recommended torque is applied using a torque wrench and then the recommended angle is added according to the protractor scale. Example: a 90° protractor tightening means that the joint is tightened a further 1/4 turn in one operation after the stated tightening torque has been applied.

Lock nuts

Do not re-use lock nuts that have been removed during disassembly operations as these have reduced service life when re-used - use new nuts when assembling or reinstalling. For lock nuts with a plastic insert such as Nylock® the tightening torque stated in the table is reduced if the Nylock® nut has the same head height as a standard hexagonal nut without plastic insert. Reduce the tightening torque by 25% for bolt size 8 mm or larger. Where Nylock® nuts are higher, or of the same height as a standard hexagonal nut, the tightening torques given in the table apply.

Strength classes

Bolts and nuts are divided up into different classes of strength; the class is indicated by the number on the bolt head. A high number indicates stronger material, for example a bolt marked 10-9 indicates a higher strength than one marked 8-8. It is therefore important that bolts removed during the disassembly of a bolted joint must be reinstalled in their original position when assembling the joint. If a bolt must be replaced check in the replacement parts catalogue to make sure the correct bolt is used.

Sealant

A number of sealants and locking liquids are used on the engines. The agents have varying properties and are used for different types of jointing strengths, operating temperature ranges, resistance to oil and other chemicals and for the different materials and gap sizes in the engines.

To ensure service work is correctly carried out it is important that the correct sealant and locking fluid type is used on the joint where the agents are required.

In this Volvo Penta Workshop Manual the user will find that each section where these agents are applied in production states which type was used on the engine.

During service operations use the same agent or an alternative from a different manufacturer.

Make sure that mating surfaces are dry and free from oil, grease, paint and anti-corrosion agent before applying sealant or locking fluid. Always follow the manufacturer's instructions for use regarding temperature range, curing time and any other instructions for the product.

Two different basic types of agent are used on the engine and these are:

RTV agent (Room temperature vulcanizing). Used for gaskets, sealing gasket joints or coating gaskets. RTV is visible when a part has been disassembled; old RTV must be removed before resealing the joint.

The following RTV agents are mentioned in the Service Manual: Loctite® 574, Volvo Penta P/N 840879-1, Permatex® No. 3, Volvo Penta P/N 1161099-5, Permatex® Nr 77. Old sealant can be removed using methylated spirits in all cases.

Anaerobic agents. These agents cure in an absence of air. They are used when two solid parts, for example cast components, are installed face-to-face without a gasket. They are also commonly used to secure plugs, threads in stud bolts, cocks, oil pressure switches and so on. The cured material is glass-like and it is therefore colored to make it visible. Cured anaerobic agents are extremely resistant to solvents and the old agent cannot be removed. When reinstalling the part is carefully degreased and then new sealant is applied.

The following anaerobic agents are mentioned in the Workshop Manual: Loctite® 572 (white), Loctite® 241 (blue).

Note: Loctite® is the registered trademark of Loctite Corparation, Permatex® the registered trademark of the Permatex Corporation.

Safety rules for fluorocarbon rubber

Fluorocarbon rubber is a common material in seal rings for shafts, and in O-rings, for example.

When fluorocarbon rubber is subjected to high temperatures (above 300°C/572°F), **hydrofluoric acid** can be formed, which is highly corrosive. Skin contact can give severe chemical burns. Splashes in your eyes can give severe chemical burns. If you breathe in the fumes, your lungs can be permanently damaged.

⚠ **WARNING!** Be very careful when working on engines which have been exposed to high temperatures, e.g. overheating during a seizure or fire. Seals must never be cut with an oxyacetylene torch, or be burned up afterwards in an uncontrolled manner.

- Always use gloves made of chloroprene rubber (gloves for handling chemicals) and protective goggles.
- Handle the removed seal in the same way as corrosive acid. All residue, including ash, can be highly corrosive. Never use compressed air to blow anything clean.
- Put the remains in a plastic box which is sealed and provided with a warning label. Wash the gloves under running water before removing them.

The following seals are probably made from fluorocarbon rubber:

Seal rings for the crankshaft, camshaft, intermediate shafts.

O-rings irrespective of where they are installed. O-rings for cylinder liner sealing are almost always made from fluorocarbon rubber.

Note that seals which have not been subjected to high temperature can be handled normally.

Technical data

General

	MD2010	MD2020	MD2030	M D2040
Engine designation				
Number of cylinders	2	3	3	3
Cylinder diameter	67 mm	67 mm	75 mm	84 mm
	(2.637 in)	(2.637 in)	(2.952 in)	(3.307 in)
Stroke length	64 mm	64 mm	72 mm	90 mm
	(2.519 in)	(2.519 in)	(2.834 in)	(3.543 in)
Swept volume, total	0.45 litres	0.68 litres	0.95 litres	1.50 litres
	(27.46 cu.in)	(41.49 cu.in)	(57.97 cu.in)	(91.53 cu.in)
Power, see sales literature				
Idling speed	850 ±25 rpm	850 ±25 rpm	850 ±25 rpm	850 ±25 rpm
Deregulation speed/high idling	3900 ±25 rpm	3900 ±25 rpm	3900 ±25 rpm	3900 ±25 rpm
Compression ratio	23.5:1	23.5:1	23:1	22:1
Compression pressure with starter motor speed	>3000 kPa	>3000 kPa	>3000 kPa	>3000 kPa
	(>435 psi)	(>435 psi)	(>435 psi)	(>435 psi)
Firing order (cyl. No. 2 and 3 closest to flywheel)	1-2	1-2-3	1-2-3	1-2-3
Direction of rotation see from front	Clockwise	Clockwise	Clockwise	Clockwise
Max. permissible angle backwards during operation	$20°$	$20°$	$20°$	$20°$
Max. side angle during operation	$30°$	$30°$	$30°$	$30°$
Valve clearance, idle cold engine: inlet and outlet	0.20 mm	0.20 mm	0.20 mm	0.20 mm
	(.0078 in)	(.0078 in)	(.0078 in)	(.0078 in)
Weight, engine without oil and water	98 kg	116 kg	129 kg	179 kg
	(215.9lb)	(255.5lb)	(284.2lb)	(394.3 lb)
Max. permissible counter pressure in exhaust pipe..	20 kPa	20 kPa	20 kPa	20 kPa
	(2.9 psi)	(2.9 psi)	(2.9 psi)	(2.9 psi)

Pistons

	MD2010 M D2020	M D2030	M D2040
Material	Aluminium alloy	Aluminium alloy	Aluminium alloy
Height, total in mm	59.045-59.095	65.575-65.625	87.66-87.74
	(2.324-2.326 in)	(2.581-2.583 in)	(3.451-3.454 in)
Height from gudgeon pin centre to piston top in mm	33.045-33.095	35.575-35.625	47.66-47.74
	(1.300-1.302 in)	(1.400-1.402 in)	(1.876-1.879 in)
Piston clearance in mm:	0.048-0.082	0.0425-0.0665	0.038-0.072
	(.0018-.0032 in)	(.0016-.0026 in)	(.0014-.0028 in)
Front marking*, MD2010, MD2020, MD2030, MD2040		The arrow alt. "F" mark on piston top should be turned forwards	The "SHIBAURA" mark in the piston should be turned forwards

* The pistons for certain engines also have an arrow in front of the gudgeon pin hole which should point forwards.

Piston rings

	MD2010 M D2020	M D2030	M D2040
Compression rings:			
Number	2	2	2
Top compression ring, height in mm	1.47-1.49	1.47-1.49	1.97-1.99
	(0578-.0586 in)	(.0578-.0586 in)	(.0775-.0783 in)
2nd compression ring, height in mm	1.47-1.49	1.97-1.99	1.47-1.49
	(.0578-.0586 in)	(.0775-.0783 in)	(.0578-.0586 in)
Oil ring:			
Number	1	1	1
Height in mm	2.97-2.99	3.97-3.99	3.90-3.98
	(.01169-1177 in)	(.01562-.1570 in)	(.1535-.1566 in)

technical data

	MD2010 M D2020	M D2030	M D2040
Piston ring gap in cylinder measured in mm,			
top compression ring	0.13-0.25 (.0051-.0098 in)	0.15-0.27 (.0059-.0106 in)	0.20-0.35 (.0078-.0137 in)
2nd compression ring	0.10-0.22 (.0039-.0118 in)	0.12-0.24 (.0047-.0094 in)	0.20-0.40 (.0078-.0157 in)
Oil ring	0.10-0.30 (.0039-.0118 in)	0.20-0.35 (.0078-.0137 in)	0.20-0.40 (.0078-.0157 in)
Piston ring clearance in groove measured in mm			
top compression ring	0.06-0.10 (.0023-.0039 in)	0.06-0.10 (.0023-.0039 in)	0.065-0.110 (.0025-.0043 in)
2nd compression ring	0.05-0.09 (.0019-.0035 in)	0.05-0.09 (.0019-.0035 in)	0.013-0.035 (.0005-.0013 in)
oil ring	0.02-0.06 (.0007-.0023 in)	0.02-0.06 (.0007-.0023 in)	0.030-0.130 (.0011-.0051 in)

Gudgeons pins

	MD2010 M D2020	M D2030	MD2040
Clearance, gudgeon pin - gudgeon bushing in mm	0.013-0.030 (.0005-.0011 in)	0.006-0.023 (.0002-.0009 in)	0.010-0.027 (.0003-.0005 in)
Gudgeon pin - gudgeon pin hole in mm	-0.004- +0.008 (-.0001- +.0003 in)	-0.004- +0.006 (-.0001-+.0002 in)	-0.001- +0.011 (-.00003- +.0004 in)
Gudgeon pin diameter in mm	18.996-19.002 (.7478-.7481 in)	20.998-21.002 (.8266-.8268 in)	27.994-28.000 (1.1021-1.1023 in)
Gudgeon bushing's int. diameter in mm	19.015-19.026 (.7486-.7490 in)	21.010-21.021 (.8271-.8275 in)	28.010-28.021 (1.1027-1.1031 in)
Gudgeon pin hole's diameter in piston in mm	18.998-19.004 (.7479-7481 in)	20.998-21.004 (.8266-.8269 in)	27.999-28.005 (1.1023-1.1025 in)

Cylinder head

	M D2010 M D2020	MD2030	MD2040
Height in mm	54.9-55.1 (2.161-2.169 in)	64.6-65.4 (2.543-2.574 in)	69.7-70.3 (2.744-2.767 in)
Valve seats (inlet outlet)			
Inlet, diameter in mm	25.35-25.45 (.9980-1.001 in)	30.35-30.45 (1.194-1.198 in)	36.35-36.45 (1.431-1.435 in)
Outlet diameter in mm	21.85-21.95 (.8602-.8641 in)	26.85-26.95 (1.0570-1.0610 in)	32.35-32.45 (1.2736-1.2775 in)
Depth in mm	2.05-2.15 (.0807-.0846 in)	2.25-2.35 (.0885-.0925 in)	2.05-2.15 (.0807-.0846 in)

Crankshaft with bearing

	MD2010	M D2020	M D2030	M D2040
(Replaceable bearing cups for main and big end bearings)				
Crankshaft, axial clearance in mm	0.1-0.3 (.0039-.0118 in)	0.1 -0.3 (.0039-.0118 in)	0.05-0.30 (.0019-.0118 in)	0.1-0.4 (.0039-.0157 in)
Main bearing, radial clearance in mm, No. 1	0.035-0.072 (.0013-.0028 in)	0.035-0.072 (.0013-.0028 in)	0.039-0.106 (.0015-.0041 in)	0.044-0.116 (.0017-.0045 in)
No. 2	0.055-0.092 (.0021-.0036 in)	0.035-0.072 (.0013-.0028 in)	0.039-0.106 (.0015-.0041 in)	0.044-0.116 (.0017-.0045 in)
No. 3		0.055-0.092 (.0021-.0036 in)	0.039-0.092 (.0015-.0036 in)	0.044-0.102 (.0017-.0040 in)

Technical data

Main bearing
Main bearing journals

			MD2010	MD2020
Diameter in mm, standard, bearing journal	No. 1		42.964-42.975	42.964-42.975
			(1.6915-1.6919 in)	(1.6915-1.6919 in)
	No. 2		45.964-45.975	42.964-42.975
			(1.8096-1.8100 in)	(1.8096-1.8100 in)
	No. 3		—	45.964-45.975
				(1.8096-1.8100 in)
undersize, No. 1	0.25 mm		42.760-42.786	42.760-42.786
	(.0098 in)		(1.6834-1.6844 in)	(1.6834-1.6844 in)
	0.50 mm		42.510-42.536	42.510-42.536
	(.0196 in)		(1.6736-1.6746 in)	(1.6736-1.6746 in)
undersize, No. 2	0.25 mm		45.764-45.790	42.760-42.786
	(.0098 in)		(1.8017-1.8027 in)	(1.6834-1.6844 in)
	0.50 mm		45.514-45.540	42.510-42.536
	(.0196 in)		(1.7918-1.7929 in)	(1.6736-1.6746 in)
undersize, No. 3	0.25 mm			45.764-45.790
	(.0098 in)			(1.8017-1.8027 in)
	0.50 mm			45.514-45.540
	(.0196 in)			(1.7918-1.7929 in)

			M D2030	MD2040
Diameter in mm, standard, bearing journal	No. 1		45.964-45.975	67.900-67.970
			(1.8096-1.8100 in)	(2.6732-2.6759 in)
	No. 2		45.964-45.975	67.900-67.970
			(1.8096-1.8100 in)	(2.6732-2.6759 in)
	No. 3		45.964-45.975	67.960-67.986
			(1.8096-1.8100 in)	(2.6755-2.6766 in)
undersize, No. 1	0.25 mm		45.854-45.934	67.650-67.720
	(.0098 in)		(1.8052-1.8084 in)	(2.6633-2.6661 in)
	0.50 mm		45.604-45.684	67.400-67.470
	(.0196 in)		(1.7954-1.7985 in)	(2.6535-2.6562 in)
undersize, No. 2	0.25 mm		45.854-45.934	67.650-67.720
	(.0098 in)		(1.8052-1.8084 in)	(2.6633-2.6661 in)
	0.50 mm		45.604-45.684	67.400-67.470
	(0196 in)		(1.7954-1.7985 in)	(2.6535-2.6562 in)
undersize, No. 3	0.25 mm	:....	45.714-45.725	67.710-67.736
	(.0098 in)		(1.7997-1.8001 in)	(2.6657-2.6667 in)
	0.50 mm		45.464-45.475	67.460-67.486
	(.0196 in)		(1.7899-1.7903 in)	(2.6559-2.6569 in)

Big-end bearing
Big-end bearing journals

	MD2010, MD2020	MD2030	M D2040
Big-end bearing, radial clearance in mm	0.031-0.068	0.035-0.083	0.035-0.085
	(.0012-.0026 in)	(.0013-.0032 in)	(.0013-.0033 in)
Bearing journal length in mm	15.65-16.55	17.70-18.60	19.70-20.60
	(.6161-.6515 in)	(.6968-.7322 in)	(.7755-.8110 in)
Diameter in mm, standard	34.964-34.975	38.964-38.975	51.964-51.975
	(1.3765-1.3769 in)	(1.5340-1.5344 in)	(2.0458-2.0463 in)
undersize, 0.25 mm	34.714-34.725	38.714-38.725	51.714-51.725
(0098 in)	(1.3666-1.3671 in)	(1.5240-1.5246 in)	(2.0359-2.0364 in)
0.50 mm	34.464-34.475	38.464-38.475	51.464-51.475
(.0196 in)	(1.3561-1.3572 in)	(1.5143-1.5147 in)	(2.0261-2.0266 in)

Technical data

Big-end bearing shells

	MD2010, MD2020	MD2030, MD2040
Thickness in mm, standard	1.484-1.497	1.482-1.495
	(.0584-.0589 in)	(.0583-.0588 in)
oversize 0.25 mm	1.609-1.622	1.607-1.620
(.0098 in)	(.0633-.0638 in)	(.0632-.0637 in)
0.50 mm	1.734-1.747	1.732-1.745
(.0196 in)	(.0682-.0687 in)	(.0681-.0687 in)

Connecting rods

	MD2010, MD2020	M D2030	M D2040
Fitted with replaceable bearing shells.			
Diameter, gudgeon bushing's bearing position	21.000-21.021	23.000-23.021	30.500-30.516
	(.8267-.8275 in)	(.9055-.9063 in)	(1.2007-1.2014 in)
Bearing shell's bearing position	19.015-19.026	21.010-21.021	28.010-28.021
	(.7486-.7490 in)	(.0827-.8275 in)	(1.1027-1.1031 in)
Gudgeon bushing	19.015-19.026	21.010-21.021	28.010-28.021
	(.7486-.7490 in)	(.8271-.8275 in)	(1.1027-1.1031 in)
Axial clearance, connecting rod -crankshaft	0.031-0.079	0.035-0.083	0.035-0.083
	(.0012-.0031 in)	(.0013-.0032 in)	(.0013-.0032 in)

Timing gears
Camshaft

	M D2010	M D2020	MD2030	MD2040
Drive	Gear wheel	Gear wheel	Gear wheel	Gear wheel
Number of bearings	3	3	3	3
Valve times:				
inlet valves open B.T.D.C	13^0	13^0	13^0	$16°$
close A.B.D.C	43^0	43^0	43^0	$40°$
outlet valves open B.B.D.C	43^0	43^0	43^0	$46°$
close A.T.D.C	13^0	13^0	13^0	10^0

Valve system
Valves

	MD2010, MD2020	M D2030	M D2040
Inlet			
Spindle diameter in mm	5.960-5.975	6.94-6.95	6.955-6.970
	(.2346-.2352 in)	(.2732-.2736 in)	(.2738-.2744 in)
Valve disc edge in mm	0.925-1.075	0.925-1.075	0.925-1.075
	(.0364-.0423 in)	(.0364-.0423 in)	(.0364-.0423 in)
Clearance in mm, valve spindle guide	0.045-0.072	0.050-0.075	0.03-0.06
	(.0017-.0028)	(.0019-.0029 in)	(.0011-.0023 in)
Seat angle in cylinder head	45^0	45^0	45^0
Valve clearance in mm, cold engine	0.20	0.20	0.20
	(.0078 in)	(.0078 in)	(.0078 in)
Outlet			
Spindle diameter in mm	5.940-5.955	6.94-6.95	6.94-6.95
	(.2338-.2344 in)	(.2732-.2736 in)	(.2732-.2736 in)
Valve disc edge in mm	0.925-1.075	0.925-1.075	0.925-1.075
	(.0364-.0423 in)	(.0364-.0423 in)	(.0364-.0423 in)
Clearance in mm, valve spindle guide	0.045-0.072	0.050-0.075	0.050-0.075
	(.0017-.0028 in)	(.0019-.0029 in)	(.0019-.0029 in)
Seat angle in cylinder head	45^0	450	45^0
Valve clearance in mm, cold engine	0.20	0.20	0.20
	(.0078 in)	(0078 in)	(.0078 in)

Technical data

Valve springs	MD2010	MD2020	MD2030	MD2040
Length in mm (in) uncompressed	33(1.299)	33(1.299)	35(1.377)	35(1.377)
with 79.4 N (58.56 ft.lbf) compression	—	—	30.4 (1.196)	30.4 (1.196)
with 67.7 N (49.93 ft.lbf) compression	28.3 (1.114)	28.3 (1.114)		—

Push rods				
Length in mm (in), total	146 (5.748)	146 (5.748)	157 (6.181)	195.8-196.2 (7.709-7.724)
Outer diameter in mm (in)	6.3 (.2480)	6.3 (.2480)	6.3 (.2480)	6.2-6.4 (.2441-0.2520)

Rocker mechanism				
Rocker shaft, diameter in mm	11.65-11.67 (.4586-.4594 in)	11.65-11.67 (.4586-.4594 in)	11.65-11.67 (.4586-.4594 in)	11.65-11.67 (.4586-.4594 in)
Clearance in mm, rocker shaft - bushing	0.032-0.068 (.0012-.0026 in)	0.032-0.068 (.0012-.0026 in)	0.032-0.068 (.0012-.0026 in)	0.032-0.068 (.0012-.0026 in)

Lubrication system

	MD2010	MD2020	MD2030	MD2040
Oil pressure in kPa, hot engine at running speed	150-500 (21.7-73 lbf/in^2)	150-500 (21.7-73 lbf/in z)	150-500 (21.7-73 lbf/in z)	150-500 (21.7-73 lbf/in^2)
Oil pressure in kPa, idling	50-150 (7.25-22 lbf/in z)	50-150 (7.25-22 lbf/in z)	50-150 (7.25-22 lbf/in z)	50-150 (7.25-22lbf/in z)
Relief valve, opening pressure in kPa	294-490 (42.6-71 lbf/in^2)	294-490 (42.6-71 lbf/in^t)	294-490 (42.6-71 lbf/in z)	245-345 (34.4-50 lbf/in z)
Oil pump:				
Clearance, inner - outer impeller	0.01-0.15 mm (.0004-.0059 in)	0.01-0.15 mm (.0004-.0059 in)	0.01-0.15 mm (.0004-.0059 in)	0.01-0.15 mm (.0004-.0059 in)
Axial clearance, impeller - cover	0.01-0.15 mm (.0004-.0059 in)	0.01-0.15 mm (.0004-.0059 in)	0.01-0.15 mm (.0004-.0059 in)	0.01-0.15 mm (.0004-.0059 in)
Oil quality as per API system	CD	CD	CD	CD
Viscosity at -5 to +50°C* (+23 to +122°F)*	SAE 15W/40. SAE 20W/50	SAE 15W/40. SAE 20W/50	SAE 15W/40. SAE 20W/50	SAE 15W/40. SAE 20W/50
Max. Oil volume incl. oil filter:				
no engine tilt (version A/B)	1.8 litres (1.9 US quarts)	3.4 litres (3.6 US quarts)	4.3 litres (4.5 US quarts)	6.4 litres (6.7 US quarts)
no engine tilt (version C)	1.9 litres (2.0 US quarts)	2.8 litres (3.0 US quarts)	3.5 litres (3.7 US quarts)	5.7 litres (6.0 US quarts)
Min. Oil volume incl. oil filter:				
no engine tilt (version A/B)	1.5 litres (1.6 US quarts)	3.0 litres (3.2 US quarts)	3.2 litres (3.4 US quarts)	5.5 litres (5.8 US quarts)
no engine tilt (version C)	1.3 litres (1.7 US quarts)	2.1 litres (2.2 US quarts)	2.7 litres (2.9 US quarts)	4.5 litres (4.8 US quarts)

* Note: Temperatures with stable ambient temperature.

Fuelsystem

	MD2010	MD2020	MD2030	MD2040
Injection sequence	1-2	1-2-3	1-2-3	1-2-3
Feed pump max. induction height in m (ft)	0.8 (2.62)	0.8 (2.62)	0.8 (2.62)	0.8 (2.62)
Feed pressure in kPa (lbf/in z)	15-25 (2.1-3.6)	15-25 (2.1-3.6)	15-25 (2.1-3.6)	15-25 (2.1-3.6)

Injection pump

	M D2010	M D2020	MD2030	MD2040
Start of injection, crankshaft position	25.5° ±1° B.T.D.C	25.5° +1° B.T.D.C[1], 27.7° ±1° B.T.D. C[2]	22.51±10 B.T.D. C[3], 21.5°±1° B.T.D.C[4]	21.0° ±10 B.T.D.C[5], 19.0°±1° B.T.D. C[6,7]
Pump element, diameter in mm (in)	4.5 (.1771)	4.5 (.1771)	5.5 (.2165)	5.5 (.2165)
stroke length in mm (in)	6(.2362)	6(.2362)	6(.2362)	7(.2755)

[1] up to and including engine number 5101311299
[2] from engine number 5101311300
[3] up to and including engine number 510101938
[4] from engine number 510101939
[5] MD2040A/B product number 868748
[6] MD2040B product number 868778
[7] MD2040C

Technical data

Injector

	MD2010	MD2020	MD2030	MD2040
Opening pressure (checking)	11.3-12.3 MPa 115-125 kp/cm^2 1639-1784 lbf/in^2	11.3-12.3 MPa 115-125 kp/cm^2 1639-1784 lbf/in^2	11.3-12.3 MPa 115-125 kp/cm^2 1639-1784 lbf/in^2	15.2-16.2 MPa 155-165 kp/cm^2 2205-2347 lbf/in^2
Opening pressure (adjustment)	11.8 MPa 120 kp/cm^2 1711 lbf/int	11.8 MPa 120 kp/cm^2 1711 lbf/int	11.8 MPa 120 kp/cm^2 1711 lbf/int	15.7 MPa 160 kp/cm^2 2276 lbf/int
Needle valve, diameter	3.5 mm (0.1378 in)	3.5 mm (0.1378 in)	6 mm (0.2362 in)	4mm (0.1575 in)
Journal diameter	1 mm (0.0394 in)	1 mm (0.0394 in)	1 mm (0.0394 in)	1 mm (0.0394 in)
Jet angle	4°	4°	4°	40

Cooling system

	MD2010	MD2020	MD2030	MD2040
Type	Overpressure, closed cooling system			
Fresh water system volume, approx (vers. A/B)	2.1 litres 2.2 US quarts	3.0 litres 3.2 US quarts	4.0 litres 4.2 US quarts	6.9 litres 7.3 US quarts
Fresh water system volume, approx (vers. C)	2.3 litres 2.4 US quarts	2.9 litres 3.1 US quarts	4.5 litres 4.8 US quarts	6.7 litres 7.1 US quarts
Thermostat, number	1 st	1st	1st	1 st
Thermostat begins to open at	75° ±2°C (167° ±4°F)	75° ±2°C (167° ±4°F)	82° ±2°C (179° ±4°F)	82° ±2°C (179° ±4°F)
fully open at	87°C (189°F)	87°C (189°F)	95°C (203°F)	95°C (203°F)
Thermostat valve's lifting height	6 mm (0.2362 in)	6mm (0.2362 in)	8 mm (0.3150 in)	8 mm (0.3150 in)

Electrical system

	M D2010	MD2020	MD2030	MD2040
System voltage	12V	12V	12V	12V
Fuses	15A	15A	15A	15A
Battery capacity (starter battery)	70 Ah	70 Ah	70 Ah	70 Ah
Glow plug:				
rated voltage	10.5V	10.5V	10.5V	10.5V
current	6.9 A	6.9 A	6.9 A	6.9 A

Alternator

	M D2010	MD2020	MD2030	MD2040
Output voltage at +20°C (+68°F)	14.2 ±0.15 V	14.2 ±0.15 V	14.2 ±0.15 V	14.2 ±0.15 V
Max. current	60 A	60 A	60 A	60 A
Power approx	840 W	840 W	840 W	840 W
Suppressor capacitor	2.2 µF	2.2 hF	2.2 hF	2.2 µF
Voltage regulator type	YV 77	YV 77	YV 77	YV 77

Starter motor

	M D2010	MD2020	MD2030	MD2040
Starter motor, power approx	0.7 kW	0.7 kW	1.2 kW	2.0 kW
Engine speed* with connected starter motor, approx	340 rpm	300 rpm	285 rpm	265 rpm

Note: refers to engine with timing gears and at approx. +20°C (+68°F).

Technical data

Wear tolerances

Note: Unless otherwise stated the given values refer to all engines.

General

Compression pressure at starter motor speed (min. 200 rpm) ....   min. 25 kp/cm^2 (355.6 lbf/int)

Pistons

Piston clearance   max. 0.25 mm (.0098 in)

Piston rings

Piston ring clearance in groove:
Compression rings   max. 0.25 mm (.0098 in)
Oil ring   max. 0.15 mm (.0059 in)
Piston ring gap in cylinder   max. 1.0 mm (.0393 in)

Gudgeon pins

Gudgeon pin diameter:
MD2010. MD2020   min. 18.98 mm (.7472 in)
MD2030   min. 20.98 mm (.8259 in)
MD2040   min. 27.98 mm (1.1015 in)
Clearance, gudgeon pin - bushing   max. 0.08 mm (.0031 in)
        gudgeon pin - hole   max. 0.02 mm (.0007 in)

Cylinder head

Distortion   max. 0.12 mm (.0047 in)

Cylinder block

Distortion (top plane)   max. 0.12 mm (.0047 in)
Cylinder diameter
MD2010. MD2020   max. 67.2 mm (2.6456 in)
  0.2 mm (.00787 in) oversize   max. 67.7 mm (2.6653 in)
  0.5 mm (.01969 in) oversize   max. 68.2 mm (2.6850 in)
MD2030   max. 75.2 mm (2.9606 in)
  0.5 mm (.01969 in) oversize   max. 75.7 mm (2.9803 in)
  1.0 mm (.03937 in) oversize   max. 76.2 mm (3.0000 in)
MD2040   max. 84.2 mm (3.3149 in)
  0.5 mm (.01969 in) oversize   max. 84.7 mm (3.3346 in)
  1.0 mm (.03937 in) oversize   max. 85.2 mm (3.3543 in)

Technical data

Crankshaft

Curvature   max. 0.06 mm (.00236 in)

Connecting rods

Linearity, deviation on 100 mm (3.937 in) measured length   max. 0.15 mm (.00590 in)
Distortion on 100 mm (3.937 in) measured length   max. 0.2 mm (.00787 in)
Axial clearance, crankshaft - connecting rod   max. 0.7 mm (.02755 in)

Valves

Max. valve clearance*, inlet and outlet (cold engine)   max. 0.5 mm (.01968 in)
* Maximum permitted valve clearance before adjustment must be carried out

Starter motor

Commutator diameter:
MD2010, MD2020, MD2040   min. 31 mm (1.2204 in)
MD2030   min. 40 mm (1.5748 in)
Brush length   min. 11.5 mm (.4527 in)
Brush spring tension MD2010, MD2020, MD2040   min. 8.8 N (2.0 lbf)
Brush spring tension MD2030   min. 13.7 N (3.0 lbf)

Technical data

Tightening torque in Nm (ft.lbf)

	MD 2010 / MD 2020	MD 2030	MD 2040
Cylinder head*	35-40 (25.8-29.5)	50-53 (36.9-39.1)	90-95 (66.4-70.1)
Main bearing:			
top to bottom bearing cap (steel)	25-30 (18.4-22.1)	25-30 (18.4-22.1)	50-55 (36.9-40.5)
(aluminium)	20-25 (14.7-18.4)	20-25 (14.7-18.4)	
Main bearing cap to cylinder block	25-30 (18.4-22.1)	25-30 (18.4-22.1)	50-55 (36.9-40.5) **
			25-30 (18.4-22.1) ***
Big-end bearing	21-26 (15.5-19.2)	30-35 (22.1-25.8)	50-55 (36.9-40.5)
End-plate/flywheel housing	13-17 (9.6-12.5)	47-55 (34.7-40.6)	13-17 (9.6-12.5)
Flywheel housing	24-29 (17.7-21.4)	24-29 (17.7-21.4)	24-29 (17.7-21.4)
Flywheel	70-80 (51.6-59.0)	60-70 (44.3-51.6)	60-70 (44.3-51.6)
Flexible coupling	9-12 (6.6-8.8)	9-12 (6.6-8.8)	9-12 (6.6-8.8)
Adapter plate for flywheel housing	24-29 (17.7-21.4)	24-29 (17.7-21.4)	24-29 (17.7-21.4)
Suction strainer, oil pump	9-13 (6.6-9.6)	9-13 (6.6-9.6)	9-13 (6.6-9.6)
Bottom plate	9-12 (6.6-8.6)	9-12 (6.6-8.6)	9-12 (6.6-8.6)
Sump	9-13 (6.6-9.6)	9-13 (6.6-9.6)	9-13 (6.6-9.6)
Drain plug, sump	30-40 (22.1-29.5)	30-40 (22.1-29.5)	30-40 (22.1-29.5)
Timing gear casing	9-12 (6.6-8.6)	9-12 (6.6-8.6)	9-12 (6.6-8.6)
Crankshaft pulley	90-100 (66-74)	120-130 (86-96)	280-340 (206-250)
Injection pump	9-13 (6.6-9.6)	9-13 (6.6-9.6)	9-13 (6.6-9.6)
Bearing bracket, rocker shaft	20-25 (14.7-18.4)	20-25 (14.7-18.4)	20-25 (14.7-18.4)
Valve cover	10-12 (7.4-8.6)	10-12 (7.4-8.6)	8-12 (5.9-8.6
Pressure oil pipe (cylinder block-cylinder head)	10-13 (7.4-9.6)	10-13 (7.4-9.6)	10-13 (7.4-9.6)
Injector	60-70 (44.3-51.6)	80-85 (59.0-62.7)	60-70 (44.3-51.6)
Delivery pipe	20-25 (14.7-18.4)	20-25 (14.7-18.4)	15-25 (11.0-18.4)
Pressure valve holder	35-39 (25.8-28.8)	40-45 (29.5-33.2)	40-45 (29.5-33.2)
Relief valve	60-70 (44.3-51.6)	60-70 (44.3-51.6)	60-70 (44.3-51.6)
Lock screw (max. fuel volume)	20-25 (14.7-18.4)	20-25 (14.7-18.4)	20-25 (14.7-18.4)
Lock screw (speed)	13-17 (9.6-12.5)	13-17 (9.6-12.5)	13-17 (9.6-12.5)
Glow plug	15-20 (11.0-14.7)	15-20 (11.0-14.7)	15¹ 2'76"(11.0-14.7)
Oil pressure relay	15-20 (11.0-14.7)	15-20 (11.0-14.7)	15-20 (11.0-14.7)
Refrigerant temperature relay	25-30 (18.4-22.1)	25-30 (18.4-22.1)	25-30 (18.4-22.1)
Oil pressure sensor	15-20 (11.0-14.7)	15-20 (11.0-14.7)	15-20 (11.0-14.7)
Refrigerant temperature sensor	15-20 (11.0-14.7)	15-20 (11.0-14.7)	15-20 (11.0-14.7)

The tightening torque given under respective engine is the final tightening torque.
The cylinder head should be tightened in three stages and in the correct sequence.
See tightening torque diagram on page 32.
Grease in the cylinder head screw threads with grease containing molybdenum disulphide.
** Hexagonal screws
Rear cap (socket head screws)

Special tools

Note. If necessary, the workshop should be equipped with 2 deep (minimum 80 mm) hexagonal sockets, 22 mm and 27mm, for removing the injectors. These sockets can be obtained from a well stocked tool supplier and are not stocked by Volvo Penta.

885224-6   Engine fixture. The tool should be supplemented with 4 pcs pin screws 479971-4, 4 pcs nuts 971095-5, 4 pcs screws 970964-3 (M10x140), 4 pcs screws 955311-6 (M8x140), 4 pcs washers 960148-5 (M10), 4 pcs washers 960141-0 (M8) and the arms from engine fixture 885050-5.

9992520-8   Overhaul stand

856927-9   Measuring plastic (disposable item)

9510060-8   Multimeter

9999179-6   Key for dismantling of fuel and oil filters.

885251-9   Adapter for measuring compression pressure MD2030.

885252-7   Adapter for measuring compression pressure MD2010, MD2020 and MD2040.

Presentation

General

The engines are in-line, 4-stroke, marine diesel engines fitted with top valves. MD2010 has two cylinders, while MD2020, MD2030 and MD2040 have three cylinders.

The engines are of the pre-chamber type and equipped with glow plugs which are activated before and during starting.

The engines are fitted with thermostat regulated fresh water cooling. The cooling system is divided into a fresh water and a sea water system. The sea water cools the fresh water system via a heat exchanger.

Lubricating takes place by means of an oil pressure system where an oil pump presses oil to all the lubrication point. The oil system is provided with a replaceable oil filter of the full-flow type.

The fuel system is protected from impurities by a replaceable fine filter.

Design differences, engine versions

This Workshop Manual applies to all engines MD2010-2040 A, B, C

The most important differences are:

MD2010-40A ≠ MD2010-40B

MD2010-40B has:

- Unipolar electrical system
- The fly wheel cover and the transmission (reverse gear or S-drive) are electrically insulated from the engine

MD2010-40B = MD2010-40C

MD2010-40C has:

- Heat exchangers with improved cooling performance and extended expansion volume
- Deeper and narrower oil sump
- Reinforced generator mountings for 2010 and 2020
- Common oil filter for 2010-40

Positioning of rating plates

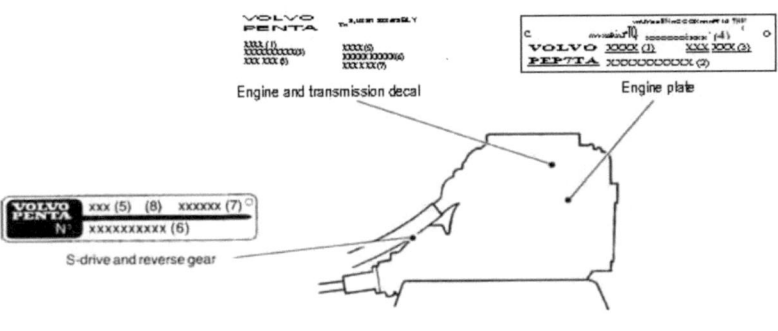

Engine and transmission decal

Engine plate

S-drive and reverse gear

1. Product designation
2. Serial number
3. Product number
4. Certification number
5. Product designation
6. Serial number
7. Product number
8. Gear ratio

Presentation

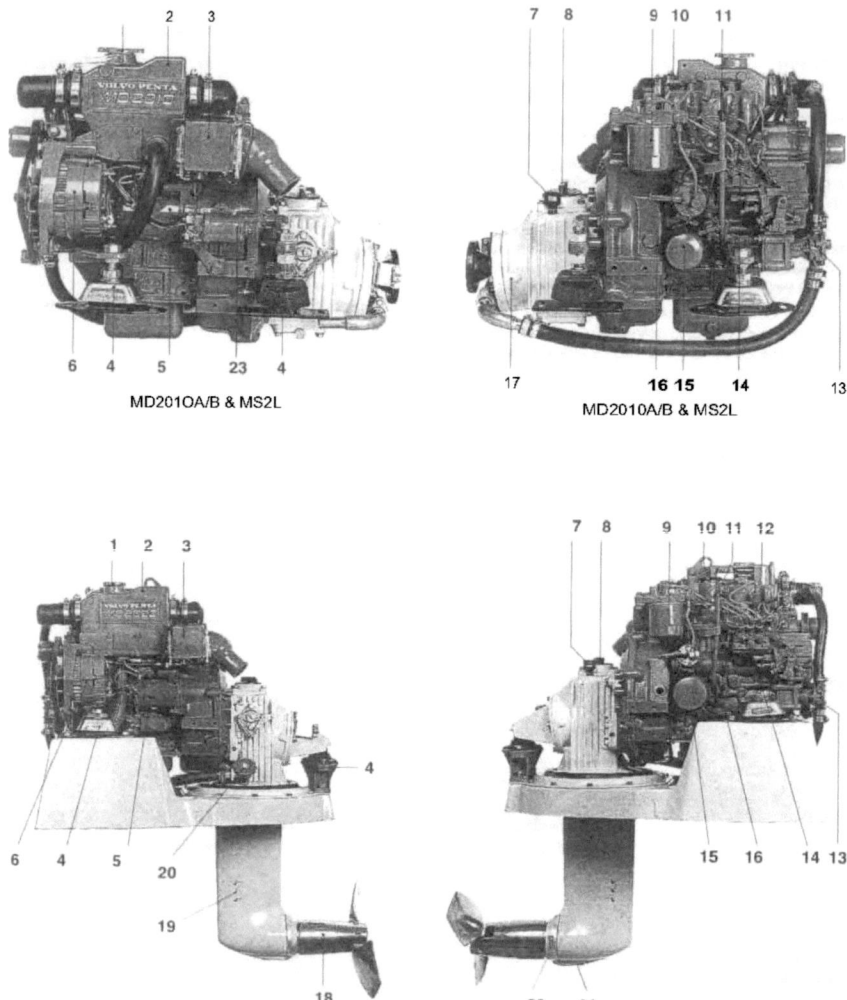

MD2010A/B & MS2L

MD2010A/B & MS2L

MD2020A/B & 120S

MD2020A/B & 120S

20

Presentation

MD2030A/B & MS2A

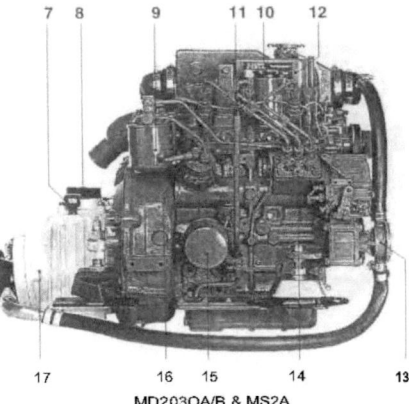

MD2030A/B & MS2A

MD2040A/B & MS2L

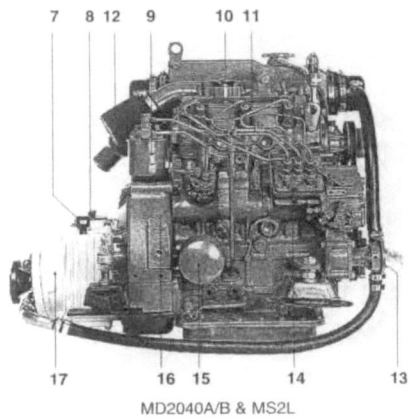

MD2040A/B & MS2L

1. Cap for replenishing of refrigerant
2. Expansion tank
3. Relay box with fuses
4. Flexible suspension
5. Starter motor
6. Alternator
7. Oil dipstick, reverse gear/S-drive
8. Cap for oil dipstick, reverse gear/S-drive
9. Fuel filter
10. Cap for oil replenishment, engine
11. Oil dipstick, engine
12. Air filter/Air intake
13. Sea water pump
14. Injection pump
15. Oil filter
16. Feed pump (with hand pump)
17. Oil cooler, reverse gear
18. Folding propeller
19. Refrigerant intake, S-drive
20. Refrigerant cock (sea water), S-drive
21. Oil drain, S-drive
22. Zinc anode (zinc ring)*
23. MD2010A-2040A: Earthing relay (for starter motor and glow plug)

Note: When running in freshwater the **magnesium anode** (magnesium ring) should be used.

Presentation

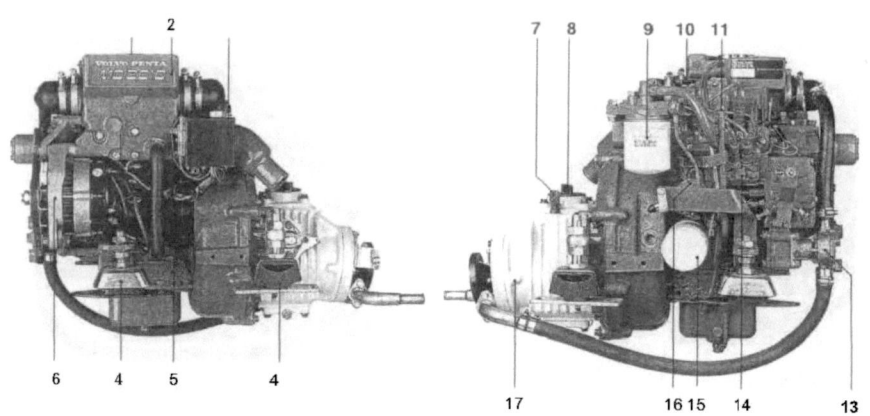

MD2010-C & MS2L

MD2010-C & MS2L

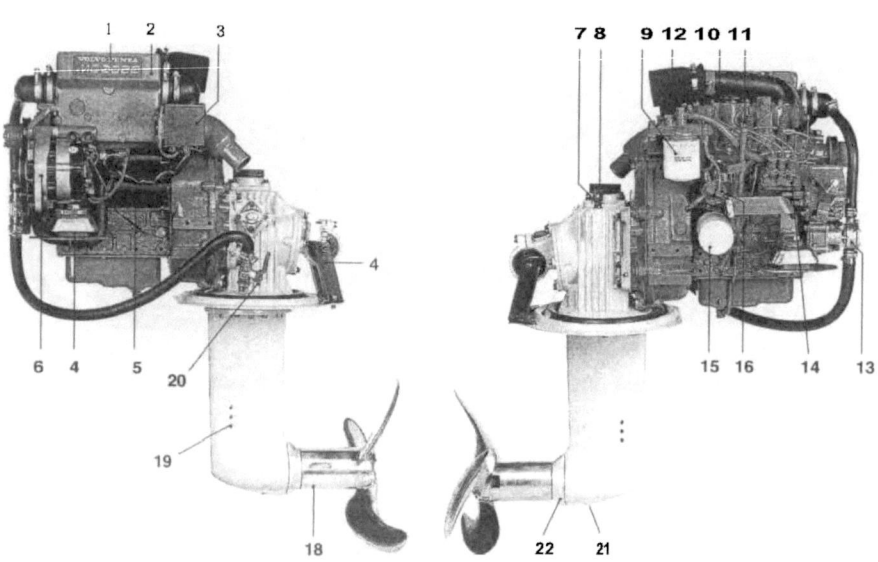

MD2020-C & 120S

MD2020-C & 120S

Presentation

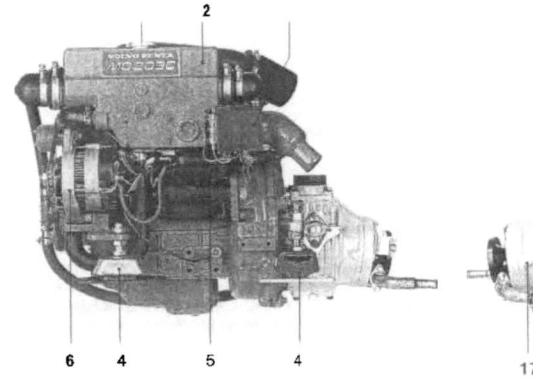

MD2030-C & MS2A

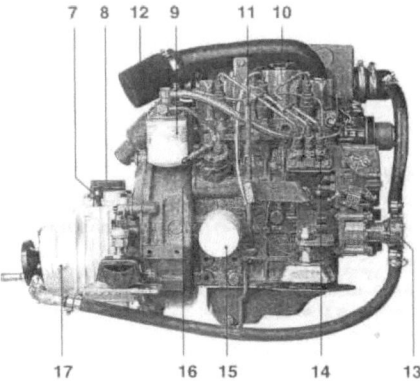

MD2030-C & MS2A

MD2040-C & MS2L

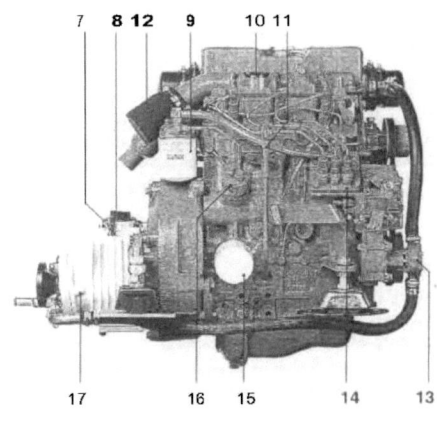

MD2040-C & MS2L

1. Cap for replenishing of refrigerant
2. Expansion tank
3. Relay box with fuses
4. Flexible suspension
5. Starter motor
6. Alternator
7. Oil dipstick, reverse gear/S-drive
8. Cap for oil dipstick, reverse gear/S-drive
9. Fuel filter
10. Cap for oil replenishment, engine
11. Oil dipstick, engine
12. Air filter/Air intake
13. Sea water pump
14. Injection pump
15. Oil filter
16. Feed pump (with hand pump)
17. Oil cooler, reverse gear
18. Folding propeller
19. Refrigerant intake, S-drive
20. Refrigerant cock (sea water), S-drive
21. Oil drain, S-drive
22. Zinc anode (zinc ring)*

Note: When running in freshwater the **magnesium anode** (magnesium ring) should be used.

Engine body

Description

Cylinder head

The cylinder head is manufactured of specially alloyed cast iron. It is provided with replaceable valve seats for the inlet valves.

The cylinder head is screwed onto the cylinder block with screws. The tightening of the cylinder head should be done in three stages.

Cylinder block

The cylinder block is cast in one piece of specially alloyed cast iron.

Pistons, piston rings

The pistons are manufactured of a light-weight metal alloy. They are fitted with three piston rings (chromium-plated) - two compression rings and an oil ring.

Camshaft

The injection pump is driven from the front part of the camshaft by means of two or three separate cams (depending on the number of cylinders).

The feed pump is driven via an eccentric cam from the rear of the camshaft.

Timing gears

The timing gears consists of cylindrical gears with bevelled cogs.

The camshaft and sea water pump are driven from the crankshaft gear via an intermediate gear. The engine's oil pump is built into the intermediate wheel and is driven via this. Regulator weights are suspended in the front edge of the camshaft gear.

Crank mechanism

Crankshaft

The crankshaft is journaled in three main bearings (MD2010), or four main bearings (other engines). The axial bearing on MD2040 consists of loose thrust washers placed at the rear main bearing. On the other engines the rear main bearing cap is made of aluminium and serves as thrust washers. The crankshaft is statically and dynamically balanced and has induction hardened bearing surfaces. At the front the crankshaft is fitted with a key joint and at the rear with a flange on which the flywheel is attached.

Main and big-end bearings

The main and big-end bearings consist of steel shells lined with bearing metal. The bearings are precision milled and ready for installation. Two oversizes are available as spare parts.

Note: The thrust washers for the crankshaft's axial bearing are not available in oversize.

Connecting rods

The connecting rods have I-sections. The piston bolt end is through-drilled for lubrication of the gudgeon pin.

Flywheel

The flywheel is screwed on a flange on the rear of the crankshaft. It is statically balanced and fully processed. The starter ring is shrunk onto the flywheel.

A flexible coupling with damper element of rubber is screwed on the flywheel. The coupling transfers the force to the reverse gear/S-drive.

Engine body

Repair instructions
Cylinder head
Dismantling of cylinder head

1. Remove both battery leads. Close the fuel cocks.

2. Close the bottom valve and drain off the water in the sea and fresh water system.

3. Release the hose to the heat exchanger from the sea water pump. Release the exhaust pipe from the exhaust hook.

4. Release the thick rubber hose under the heat exchanger. (**Note:** the hose is filled with refrigerant). Release the thin hose from the refrigerant pump.

5. MD2010, MD2020: remove the drive belt for the alternator/refrigerant pump. Remove the alternator and clamp.

6. Release the relay box from the heat exchanger housing and hang it up.

7. Release the electric cables to the oil pressure relay and to the refrigerant temperature relay and sensor (where appropriate).

8. MD2040: remove the cover at the front on the heat exchanger housing's right-hand side. Remove the spacer ring, thermostat and rubber seal.

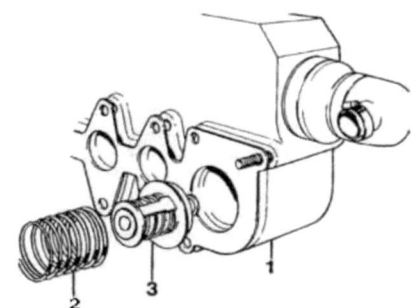

Fig. 9. Dismantling of expansion tank with heat exchanger
1. Heat exchanger complete
2. MD2010, MD2020: Spring
3. MD2010, MD2020: Thermostat

9. Remove the expansion tank complete with heat exchanger.
   MD2010, MD2020: Remove the spring, thermostat and rubber seal from the heat exchanger housing.

10. MD2010, MD2020, MD2030:
    Remove the induction manifold.
    MD2040:
    Remove the inlet pipe complete with air filter.

11. Release the delivery pipe at the injection pump and injectors. Lift off the delivery pipes together. Protect the connections from impurities.

12. Remove the nut at the top of respective injectors and lift off the fuel leak pipe.

Engine body

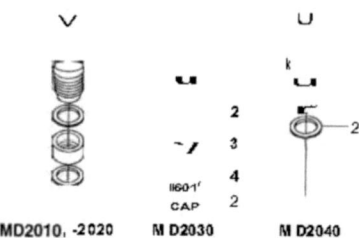

MD2010, -2020   M D2030   M D2040

Fig. 10. Dismantling of injectors
1. Injector 3. Heat shield (MD2030)
2. Copper gasket 4. Insert (MD2010-2030)

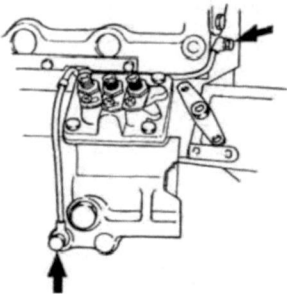

Fig. 12. Dismantling of oil pressure pipe (cylinder block - cylinder head/rocker mechanism)

13. Unscrew the injectors. Use a long socket, 80 mm.
    MD2010, MD2020, MD2030 = 22 mm
    MD2040 = 27 mm.
    Remove the copper gaskets under the injectors.
    MD2030: Remove the heat shields (3, Fig. 10).
    MD2010, MD2020, MD2030: Remove the inserts (4) and the lower copper washers.

16. Remove the oil pressure pipe between the cylinder block and cylinder head (rocker mechanism on MD2040).

17. Remove the valve cover (built together with the inlet pipe on MD2010, MD2020 and MD2030).

14. Release the electric cable to the glow plug. Remove the conductor rail and unscrew the glow plug.

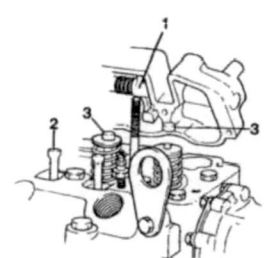

Fig. 13. Dismantling of rocker mechanism (MD2040)
1. Rocker mechanism 3. Valve caps
2. Pull rods

18. Release the nuts from the rockers' bearing brackets. Remove the rocker mechanism (1, Fig. 13) and pull rods (2). Remove the valve caps (3, MD2040) from the valve stem.

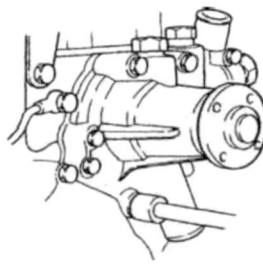

Fig. 11. Dismantling of circulation pump

15. MD2010, MD2020, MD2030: Remove the circulation pump.
    MD2030: Note. The pump must be released/removed **before** the cylinder head is released. The pump can otherwise be broken. Remove the spring and thermostat.

19. Release the cylinder head screws in several stages.
    Note: Begin in the middle of the cylinder head and release the screws in a circle outwards.
    Lift off the cylinder head.

Stripping of cylinder head

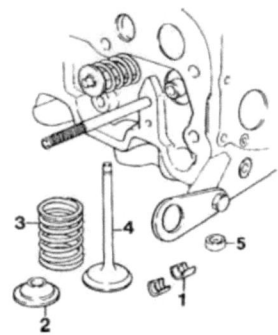

Fig. 14. Dismantling the valves
1. Valve lock
2. Valve spring washer
3. Valve spring
4. Valve
5. Valve cap*

*MD2040 and later versions of MD2010, 2020, 2030

1. Remove the valves and valve springs. Press the springs together with a valve spring tensioner and remove the valve lock. Place the valves in order in a marked valve rack. Remove the valve stem seals.

2. Clean all parts. Observe special care with the channels for oil and refrigerant.

3. Remove residual soot and impurities from the cylinder head's sealing surfaces.

   Note: Do not use use steel brush to clean the cylinder head screw threads or under the screw heads.

Inspection of cylinder head

The flatness tolerance for the cylinder head is max. 0.12 mm (.00472"). Check in six positions ("A-F" as per Fig. 15 and 16). Use a feeler gauge and a ruler the sides of which are precision rubbed as per DIN 874/Normal.

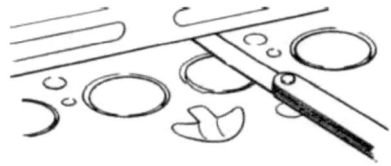

Fig. 15. Checking of cylinder head flatness

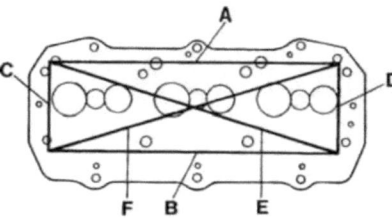

Fig. 16. Checking of cylinder head flatness

If the flatness is not within the permissible tolerance the cylinder head should be replaced. If leakage or blow marks are confirmed it is not necessary to check for flatness since the cylinder head must be replaced.

Check the valve seats and that the pin screws are tight.

For replacement of the valve seats (inlet) see next page.

Engine body

Replacement of valve seat

Grinding of valves and valve seats

1. Use a valve spring tensioner and dismantle the valve lock. Remove the valve spring washers, springs and aloes. Place the parts in the correct order in a valve rack. Remove the valve stem seals.
2. Clean the parts.

Fig. 17. A = distance between cylinder head plane and valves.

The valve seat should be replaced when the distance "A" in Fig. 17 measured with a **new** valve exceeds 1.8 mm (.0708").

1. Remove the old valve seat by heating it up with a gas jet (600-700°C / 1112-1292°F) diagonally over the seat.
   Allow the cylinder head to cool approx. 3-5 minutes in the air. Carefully tap out the seat with mandrel (check that the cylinder head is not damaged).
   Alternatively the valve seat can be milled out (check that the cylinder head is not damaged).

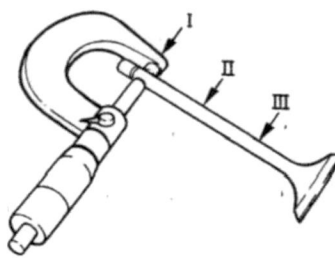

Fig. 18. Checking of valve spindle wear

Diameter mm:	Inlet	Outlet
MD2010, MD2020	5.90 mm (.2322 in)	5.90 mm (.2322 in)
MD2030, MD2040	6.89 mm (.2712 in)	6.84 mm (.2692 in)

Check the wear on the valve spindle. Measure the diameter with a micrometer at points I, II and III as per Fig. 18.

2. Clean the seat housing in the cylinder head carefully. Check the head for cracking.
3. Cool down the new seat with liquid nitrogen or the like to minus 60-70°C (140-158°F) and heat up the cylinder head to approx. 60-100°C (140-212°F).
4. Press the seat in the head. Use a hydraulic press (1000-1500 kp / 2204-3307 lbf) and suitable mandrel.
5. Work the seats to the correct angle and width.

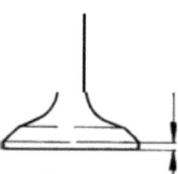

Fig. 19. Valve disc edge

4. Grind the valves in a valve grinding machine
   Grind the sealing surface as little as possible, just so that it is "clean". If the the valve disc edge after grinding is less than 0.5 mm (.019 in) the valve should be scrapped (see Fig. 19). The same applies to valves with crooked valve spindles.

Engine body

5. Check the wear on the valve guides (see "Checking of valve guides") before the valve seats are treated.

8. Fit the seals, valves, valve springs, spring washers, valve lock and valve caps. See "Assembly of cylinder head" on page 31.

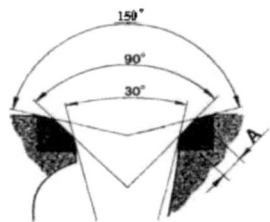

Fig. 20. Grinding of valve seat

A= Max. 2.5 mm (.0984 in)

6. Ream or grind the valve seats (Fig. 20). Grind of just enough material so that the valve seat has the right shape and a good mating surface.

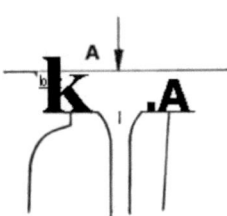

Fig. 21. Checking of valve seat

Replace the valve seat when the distance "A" in Fig. 21, measured with a new valve, exceeds 1.8 mm (.0708 in).

For replacement of the valve seat (inlet) see previous page.

New seats are grind down so that the distance between the cylinder head plane and the valve disc surface "A" is:
MD2010, MD2020: 0.70-0.90 mm (.0275-.0354 in)
MD2030, MD2040: 0.85-1.15 mm (.0334-.0452 in)

7. Grind in the valves with grinding paste and check the contact with marker dye.

Checking of valve guides*

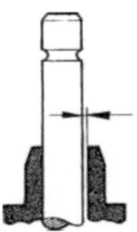

Fig. 22. Clearance, valve - valve guide (cylinder head)

Calculate the clearance between the valve spindle and valve guide.

Wear tolerances:

Inlet valve, max. clearance   0.20 mm (.0078 in)
Outlet valve, max. clearance   0.25 mm (.0098 in)

* Note: Since the valve guides are treated directly in the cylinder head this must be replaced when the clearance is excessive, even when the valve is new.

Checking of valve springs

Check that the springs do not show any signs of damage.

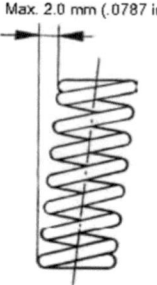

Fig. 23. Checking of linearity

Place the valve springs on a level surface and check the linearity with a st square (Fig. 23).

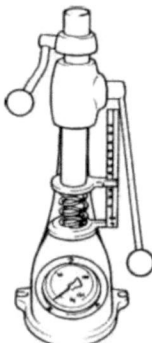

Fig. 24. Spring tester

Place the spring in a spring tester and check its length both compressed and uncompressed.

The springs should maintain the values given in "Technical data".

Renovating the rocker mechanism

1. MD2010, MD2020, MD2030: Remove the screws at the front and rear of the rocker shaft.

   MD2040: Screw in a M8 screw in the threaded hole in the front edge of the rocker shaft. Fix the screw head in a vice and pull out the rocker shaft (alt. a withdrawing tool can be used).

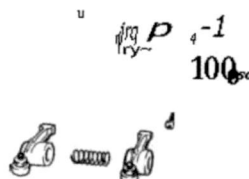

Fig. 25. Dismantling of rocker mechanism (MD2040)

2. Dismantle the rocker mechanism. Remove the rockers, springs and washers.

3. Clean the parts. Observe special care with the rocker shaft's oil channels and oil holes in the rockers.

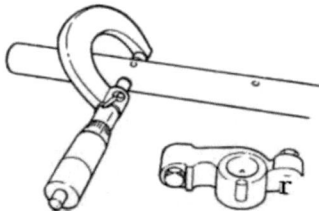

Fig. 26. Measuring of rocker shaft

4. Check the wear on the rocker shaft with a micrometer (Fig. 26). Diameter min. 11.57 mm (.4555 in).

Engine body

Fitting of cylinder head

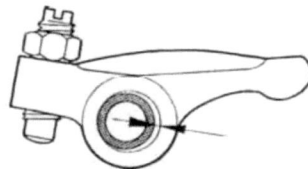

Fig. 27. Clearance rocker - rocker shaft

Fig. 28. Fitting of valve stem seals

5. Check that the rocker bearing surfaces are not out-of-round worn.

   Calculate the clearance between the rocker and shaft. The clearance must not exceed 0.2 mm (.0078 in).

   Check that the ball pin's spherical part is not deformed or worn. The threads should be undamaged on the pin and lock nut. The locknut should be in good condition.

   The mating sphere of the rockers (against the valve) must not be unevenly worn or concave. Adjustment for minor wear can be made in a grinding machine.

   Note: MD2010-2030. A new type of rocker (including valve cap) has been introduced as from engine number:

   MD2010: 5101202984
   MD2020: 5101308898
   M D2030: 5101465653

   Only the new type of rocker is available as a spare part. If one or several of the older type of rocker need to be replaced, all the rockers must be replaced at once, and valve caps installed on the valve stems.

1. Press down new valve stem seals on the valve guides.

   Note: MD2030 and MD2040 have different seals for the guides for the inlet and outlet valves.

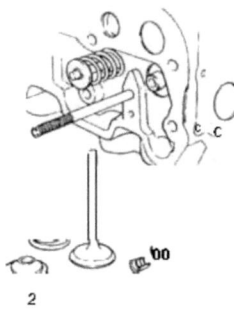

Fig. 29. Fitting of valves
1. Valve lock   3. Valve spring
2. Valve spring retainer   5. Valve cap*
4. Valve
*MD2040 and later versions of MD2010, 2020, 2030

2. The valves should be fitted in the correct order. Oil in the valve spindles and fit the valve in its guide. Place the valve spring and retainer in position and press the spring together with a valve spring tensioner. Fit the valve lock.

   Note: Observe care when fitting the valves and compressing the springs so that the valve stem seals are not damaged.

3. Fit the valve caps when all valves are fitted. (Applies to MD2040 and later versions of MD2010, MD2020, MD2030 (Please refer to the note below item 5)).

4. Fit new plugs if these have been removed.

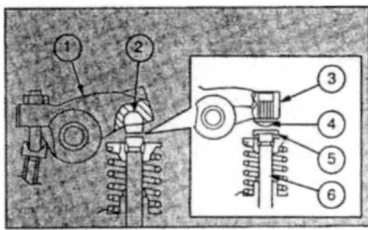

Comparison between new and old rockers
1. Earlier rocker   4. The new rocker tip
2. Earlier rocker tip   5. Valve cap
3. The new rocker   6. Valve

6. Oil in the rocker mechanism and fit the different parts.

Engine body

Fitting of cylinder head

1. Clean the surface of the cylinder head and cylinder block. Remove any rust or soot from the screw holes and threads for the cylinder head screws.
2. Fit on the new cylinder head gasket.
3. Apply grease containing molybdenum disulphide on the cylinder head screws.

   NOTE! The screws are surface treated and must not be cleaned with a steel brush.

   Note: If the cylinder head is painted the mating surfaces for cylinder head screws must be free from paint, otherwise the clamping force in the screw union will be adversely affected.
4. Check that the tubular pins (guides) are fitted in the block. Place the two rear cylinder head screws in the cylinder head and fit the head.

1st tightening

MD2010, MD2020	10 Nm (7.40 ft.lbs)
MD2030	20 Nm (14.80 ft.lbs)
MD2040	30 Nm (22.10 ft.lbs

2nd tightening

MD2010, MD2020	20 Nm (14.80 ft.lbs)
MD2030	35 Nm (25.80 ft.lbs)
MD2040	70 Nm (51.70 ft.lbs)

Final tightening

MD2010, MD2020	35-40 Nm (26-30 ft.lbs)
MD2030	50-53 Nm (37-39 ft.lbs)
MD2040	90-95 Nm (66-70 ft.lbs)

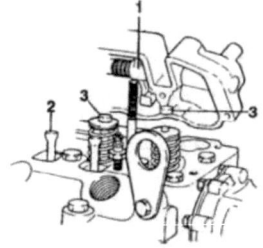

Fig. 32. Fitting of the rocker mechanism (MD2040)

6. Fit the pull rods (2), valve caps (3, MD2040 and later versions of 2010, 2020, 2030) and rocker mechanism (1).

7. Adjust the valve clearance as per directions on page 34. Fit the valve cover.

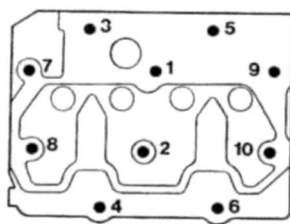

Fig. 30. Tightening diagram, MD2010

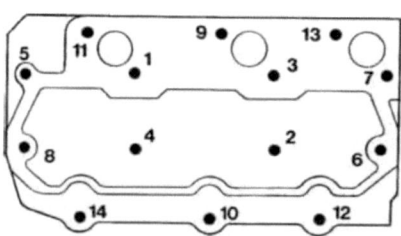

Fig. 31. Tightening diagram MD2020, MD2030, MD2040

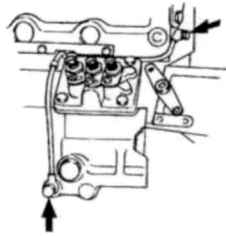

Fig. 33. Fitting of oil pressure pipe (cylinder block - cylinder head / rocker mechanism)

5. Tighten the cylinder head screws in three stages as per the following. See tightening diagrams Fig. 30-31.

8. Fit the oil pressure pipe between the block and cylinder head (rocker mechanism on MD2040).
   Tightening torque 10-13 Nm (7.4-9.6 ft.lbs).

Engine body

9. MD2010, MD2020: Fit the circulation pump.
   MD2030: Fit the circulation pump and thermostat and spring (see Fig. 35).
10. Fit the glow plug, Tightening torque: see Technical data. Fit the conductor rail and connect the electric cable.

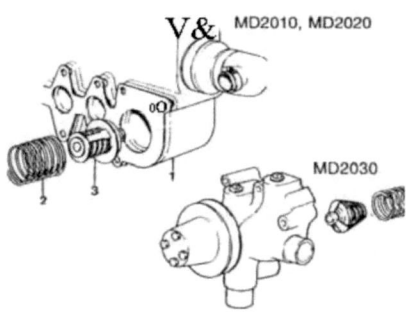

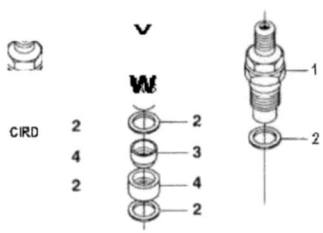

Fig. 34. Fitting of injectors

1. Injector
2. Copper gasket
3. Heat shield (MD2030)
4. Insert (MD2010-2030)

11. Fit the copper gaskets, heat shields (MD2030) and inserts (MD2010-MD2030) to the injectors as per Fig. 34.
    Fit the injectors. Use socket L=80 mm (3.15 in), key width = 22 mm (MD2010-MD2030), and 27 mm (MD2040).
    Tightening torque MD2010, MD2030, MD2040:
    60-70 Nm (44.3-51.7 ft.lbs)
    Tightening torque MD2030:
    80-85 Nm (59.0-62.7 ft.lbs).
12. Put on new copper gasket and fit the fuel leak pipe. Tighten the nuts and connect the return pipe.
13. Fit the delivery pipe complete. Tightening torque 20-25 Nm (14.8-18.4 ft.lbs).
14. MD2010, MD2020, MD2030: Fit the induction manifold.
    MD2040: Fit the inlet pipe complete with air filter.

Fig. 35. Fitting of thermostat (MD2010, MD2020, MD2030) and expansion tank.

15. MD2010, MD2020: Fit the rubber seal, thermostat (3) and spring (2) in the heat exchanger housing (1)
16. Fit the expansion tank complete with heat exchanger. Connect the hoses to the heat exchanger housing and refrigerant pump. Tighten the hose clips.

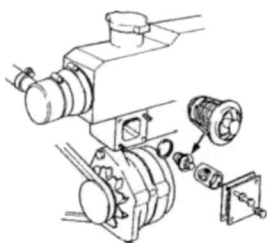

Fig. 36. Fitting of thermostat (MD2040)

17. MD2040: Fit the rubber seal, thermostat and spacer ring in the heat exchanger housing. Fit the cover over the thermostat.
18. Connect the electric cables to the oil pressure relay, and to the refrigerant temperature relay and sensor (where appropriate).

33

Engine body

19. Fit the relay box.
20. MD2010, MD2020: Fit the alternator and clamp. Fit the drive belt.

    Note: It should be possible to press in the belt approx. 10 mm (.40 in) between the pulleys.
21. Connect the hose to the sea water pump and tighten the clip. Connect the exhaust pipe.
22. Fill with refrigerant. See "Replenishment of refrigerat on page 64.
23. Connect the battery cables. Open the fuel cocks and bottom valve. Start the engine and check that no leakage occurs.

4. **MD2020. MD2030. MD2040:** Check and adjust if necessary the valve clearance for cylinder No. 1, and the clearance for the outlet valve on cylinder No. 2.

   Pull round the crankshaft 240° (2/3 turn) anti-clockwise (seen from front) and adjust the clearance for cylinder No. 3 and the clearance for the inlet valve on cylinder No. 2.

5. Clean the valve cover and fit it. Replace the seal if damaged. Test run the engine and check that no leakage occurs.

Adjusting the valves

Note! The clearance must never be checked when the engine is running.

Valve clearance (cold engine):

Inlet and outlet for all engines: 0.20 mm (.0078 in).

1. Dismantle the valve cover.
2. Turn the engine in its normal direction of rotation until both valves for cylinder No. 1 are closed (compression position). Continue turning the engine round until the marking of flywheel shows 0°.

Dismantling of piston, piston rings and connecting rod

1. Empty the cooling system and drain or syphon out the engine oil.
2. Dismantle the cylinder head. See "Dismantling of cylinder head" on page 25 and 26.

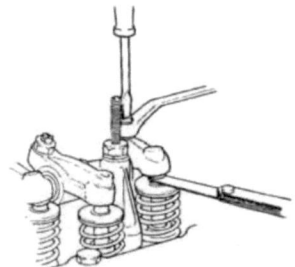

Fig. 37. Adjusting the valves

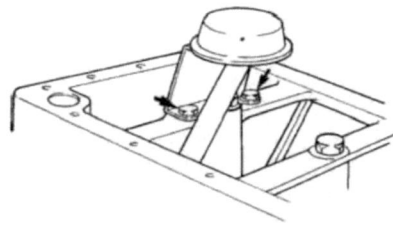

Fig. 38. Dismantling of oil strainer with induction manifold

3. **MD2010:** Check and adjust if necessary the valve clearance for cylinder No. 1.

   Pull round the crankshaft 180° (1/2 turn) clockwise (seen from front) and adjust the clearance for cylinder No. 2.

3. Remove the sump and plate` over the sump. Remove the oil pump's induction manifold.

   There is no plate on the MD2010-40C.

Engine body

4. Turn round the crankshaft until the piston in question is in the lower turning position. Dismantle the main bearing cap with lower bearing cup.

Inspection and matching of piston rings

Check the wear surfaces and sides. Black patches on the surfaces imply poor contact and indicate that it is time to change the piston rings. The oil consumption is also a critical factor as to when a piston ring should be replaced.

Check the piston ring gap (Fig. 41). Push down the ring **below the lower turning position** by means of a piston. Replace the piston ring if the gap exceeds 1.0 mm (.039 in).

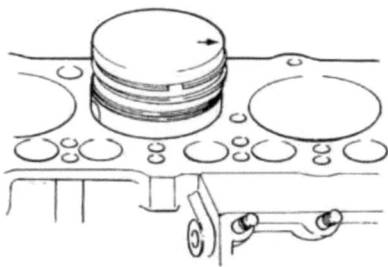

Fig. 39. Dismantling of piston

5. Place a pair of plastic hoses as protection over the connecting rod screws. Carefully tap up the connecting rod with piston far enough so that the piston rings are released from the cylinder bore. Lift off the piston together with the connecting rod.

   Note: Scrape off the soot strip in the top part of the cylinder bore to simplify dismantling.

6. Dismantle piston ring with a piston ring tongs.

Fig. 41. Checking of piston ring gap

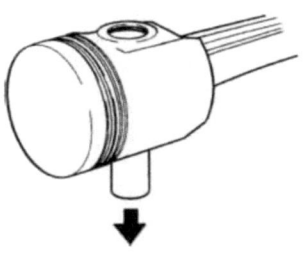

Fig. 40. Dismantling of gudgeon pin

7. Remove the circlips for the gudgeon pin and dismantle the gudgeon pin carefully with a suitable mandrel.

Piston rings should also be replaced if there is noticeable wear or out-of-roundness in the cylinders since the rings seldom have the same position as they had before dismantling.

Check the piston ring gap also on new rings.

See "Technical data" for size info.

Check the clearance in the piston ring groove. Roll the ring in its groove in the piston and measure the clearance at a number of points with a feeler gauge.

Engine body

Assembly of piston, piston rings and connecting rod

Note: Check that pistons of the correct oversize are used if the cylinders have been milled to oversize.

1. Fit one circlip in the piston.
2. Oil in the gudgeon pin and bushing.

6. Check the big-end clearance. See "Inspection of crankshaft" and "Inspection of main and big-end bearings" on pages 46 and 47.
7. Check the piston ring gap in the cylinder bore (Fig. 41 on page 35) and that the rings do not jam in the piston ring grooves.

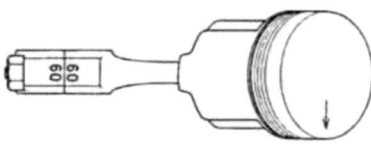

Fig. 49. Assembly of piston and connecting rod (MD2010, MD2020)

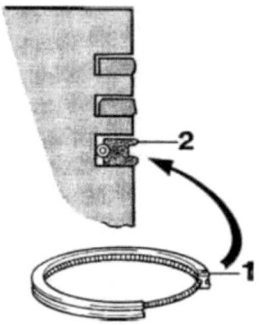

Fig. 51. Placement of piston rings
1. TOP marking
2. Oil scraper with expander spring (MD2010-2030)

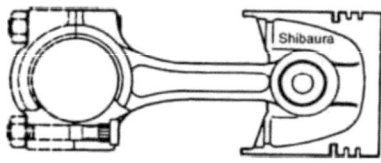

Fig. 50. Assembly of piston and connecting rod (MD2030, MD2040)

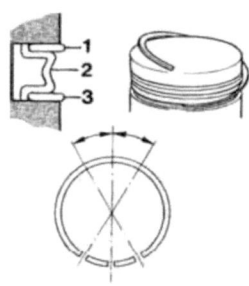

Fig. 52. Fitting of oil ring (MD2040)
1. Top scraper ring   3. Bottom scraper ring
2. Expander

3. Heat up the piston to approx. 100°C (212°F). Place the piston and connecting rod so that the markings correspond with Fig. 49 or 50.

   MD2010, MD2020: With the marking on the connecting rod's side upwards the arrow on the piston top should be turned in the same direction as per Fig. 49.

   MD2030, MD2040: The marking on the connecting rod and the "SHIBAURA" mark in the piston should be turned in the same direction as per Fig. 50.

   Push in the gudgeon pin.

   NOTE! The gudgeon pin should be able to be pressed in easily. It must not be knocked in.

4. Fit the other circlip.

5. Check that the connecting rod goes easily in the gudgeon pin bearing.

8. Fit the piston rings on the piston with a piston ring tong.

   Note: The rings should be turned as per Fig. 51.

   MD2010, MD2020, MD2030: Fit the oil ring first (with the marking turned upwards). The opening in the expander spring should be placed 180° from the oil ring gap.

MD2040: Place the expander (2, Fig. 52 on page 38) to the oil scraper rings in the piston ring groove. Check that the ends on the expander do not overlap each other. Fit the top scraper ring (1) over the the expander. Put in one end of the ring in the groove and hold it in place with your thumb. Push the ring in position with your other thumb.

Fit the lower scraper ring (3) in the same way.

Check that the scraper rings run easily in both directions and that the ends on the expander and the rings are in the correct position (Fig. 52).

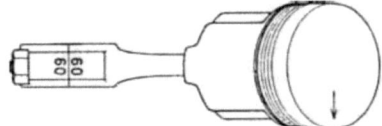

Fig. 53. Number marking on connecting rod and cap

3. Check that the marking on the piston top, alt. in the piston and on the connecting rod, correspond with Fig. 53.

   Use a piston ring compressor and fit the piston with connecting rod in the respective cylinder, beginning with cylinder No. 1 (first).

   Note: The connecting rod with the **lowest number** should be fitted first (to cylinder No. 1) and subsequently the connecting rod with the highest number closest to the flywheel.

   The connecting rod should be turned with the marking (number/colour marking) turned "towards the injection pump" (camshaft side). The arrow on the piston top alt. at the gudgeon pin hole should thereby point forwards.

Fitting of piston in cylinder

Note: After replacing a connecting rod, piston or gudgeon pin the weight difference between the connecting rod complete with piston and piston rings must not exceed 10 g (0.35 oz) between the different cylinders.

1. Lubricate the piston and piston rings with engine oil and turn the rings so that the oil penetrates the piston ring groove. Turn the piston rings so that the piston ring gaps are divided by 900 from each other.

   Note: Make sure that no piston ring gap is positioned opposite the piston bolt or at right angles to it.

   MD2040: Check that the ends on the expander and scraper rings are in the correct position (Fig. 52).

2. Place the bearing cups in their positions in the connecting rod and cap. Check that the hole in the bearing cups comes opposite the hole in the connecting rod. Oil in the crank pin with engine oil.

4. Fit the bearing cap and tighten the connecting rod screws. See "Technical data" for tightening torque.

   Note: The main bearing cap should be fitted so that the number/colour marking on the crankshaft and cap correspond (Fig. 53).
   Undamaged connecting rod screws do not need to be changed and can be re-fitted.

Engine body

Timing gears

Replacement of front crankshaft seal

The seal consists of a rubber ring and can be replaced after the crankshaft pulley has been removed. Use a universal extractor.

1. Tap in one side of the seal so that it goes on edge. Pull out the seal with a hook.

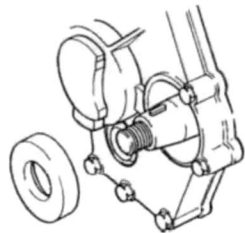

Fig. 54. Fitting of crankshaft seal

3. Oil in the new seal with fit it with a suitable mandrel.

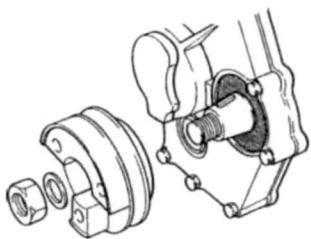

Fig. 55. Fitting of crankshaft pulley

4. Remove the fitting tool. Fit the key and crankshaft pulley.

   See Technical data for tightening torque.

Dismantling of the timing gear

Q **WARNING!** If the crankshaft and camshaft are turned without being synchronised with each other the valves can go against the pistons and be damaged.

1. Close the fuel cocks. Remove both battery leads.

2. Close the bottom valve. Release the rubber hoses to the sea water pump and drain out the water in the sea water system.

3. Remove the sea water pump.

4. Remove the drive belt for the alternator.

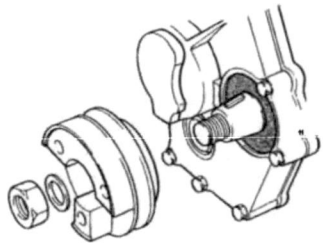

Fig. 56. Dismantling of crankshaft pulley

5. Remove the pulley from the crankshaft. Use a universal extractor (Use an adjustable spanner on the lug on the pulley as a counterhold when the nut is removed)

6. Remove the delivery pipe complete. Release the fuel house and fuel leak pipe at the injection pump.

Engine body

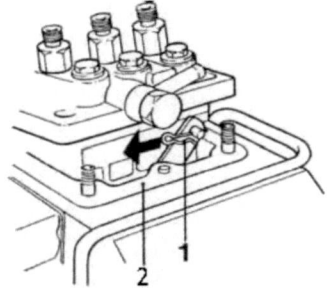

Fig. 57. Dismantling of injection pump
1. Lock pin   2. Shims

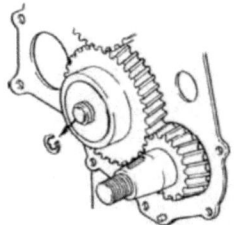

Fig. 59. Dismantling of circlip to cover for the oil pump

7. Release the injection pump. Turn the stop lever clockwise and carefully lift up the pump so that the lock pin to the regulator arm is accessible (Fig. 57).
   Remove the lock pin and release the regulator arm. Lift off the injection pump.
   NOTE! Take care off the shims under the injection pump flange.

8. Dismantle the timing gear casing.

10. Remove the circlip for the intermediate gear (Fig. 59). Take care of the sleeve washer, spring and shims.
    Lift off the gear complete with cover and oil pump.

11. Dismantle the crankshaft gear with a universal extractor.

12. If the camshaft gear is to be dismantled the camshaft must be removed complete. See under heading "Dismantling of camshaft" on page 44.

Inspection of timing gears

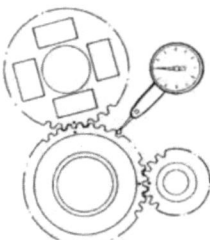

Fig. 60. Checking of gear flank clearance

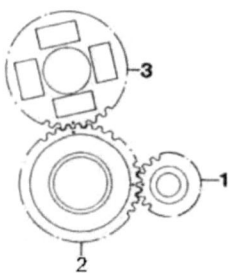

Fig. 58. Timing gears, basic setting
1. Crankshaftgear   3. Camshaftgear
2. Intermediate gear

9. Pull round the engine until the markings on the timing gears correspond.

Clean the gears and other parts of the timing gears and check them carefully. Replace gears which are heavily worn or damaged.

Check the flank clearance with a feeler gauge or a dial gauge.

Max. permissible flank clearance: 0.25 mm (.0098 in).

Note: If the flank clearance exceeds the permissible value all the the gears in the timing gears should be replaced.

Engine body

Fitting and adjustment

 WARNING! If the crankshaft and camshaft are turned without being synchronised with each other the valves can go against the pistons and be damaged.

Note: The gears in the timing gears which are of importance for adjustment are marked as follows:

Crankshaft gear - the intermediate gear is marked with a punch mark and the intermediate gear - camshaft gear with a circle opposite the tooth and tooth gap (Fig. 61).

1. Put the key in position in the crankshaft and fit the crankshaft gear.
2. Fit the camshaft complete with regulator weights. Carry out work steps to item 4 under the heading "Fitting of camshaft" on page 45.

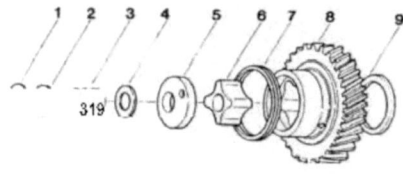

Fig. 62. Intermediate gear complete with oil pump

1. Circlip
2. Spring washer
3. Spring
4. Shims
5. Cover to oil pump
6. Inner rotor
7. Spring
8. Intermediate gear complete with outer rotor
9. Thrust washer

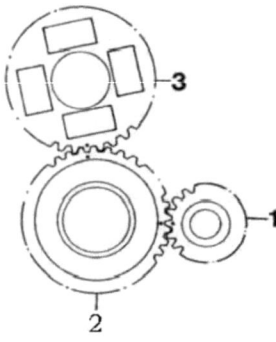

Fig. 61. Timing gears, basic setting
1. Crankshaft gear   3. Camshaft gear
2. Intermediate gear

4. Grease in the oil pump's inner rotor (6, Fig 62) and housing (outer rotor, 8).

   Fit the inner rotor and cover to the oil pump. Fit the shims, spring, spring washer and lock washer as per Fig. 62.

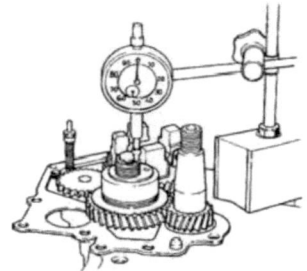

Fig. 63. Checking of oil pump's axial clearance

5. Adjust the oil pump's axial clearance to 0.10-0.15 mm (.0039-.0059 in). Shims are available in sizes 0.10; 0.15; 0.20 and 0.50 mm (.0039, .0059, .0078 and .0196 in)

3. Fit the thrust washer (9, Fig. 62) on the intermediate gear's shaft journal. Fit the intermediate gear as per the markings (Fig. 61).

   NOTE! Do not turn the crankshaft before the timing gear casing is fitted.

6. Check the crankshaft seal in the timing gear casing, and replace if necessary. See under heading "Replacement of front crankshaft seal" on page 40.

Engine body

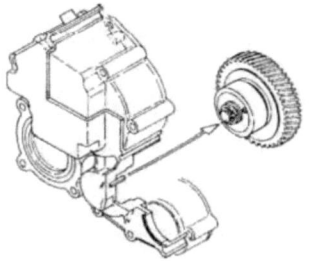

Fig. 64. Fitting of timing gear casing

7. Centre the cover in front of the oil pump.

   Note: The hole in the cover should be in the position shown in Fig. 64 (which it should if the markings on the gear wheel coincide according to Fig. 61).

8. Place the timing gear casing in position with a new gasket. Observe care so that the crankshaft seal is not damaged.

   Check that the start spring is in position in the timing gear casing and is connected to the regulator arm (link arm).

   Put in the regulator through the hole in the cylinder block.

   Note: Check that the tubular pip in the timing gear casing can engage in the hole in the oil pump cover. Turn the cover backwards and forwards and centre it in mid position.

NOTE! Make sure that the shims which were placed under the injection pump flange are replaced in position before the pump is placed in the cylinder block (applicable where the pumps has been removed).

10. Tighten the timing gear casing and injection pump.
    Tightening torque: see Technical data.

11. Check the injection start (crankshaft position) in the event that a new injection pump or complete new camshaft is fitted and if a new cylinder block is used.
    Se directions under the heading "Adjustment of injection angle" on pages 55 and 56.

12. Connect the fuel hose to the injection pump.
    Fit the delivery pipe.
    Tightening torque: see Technical data.

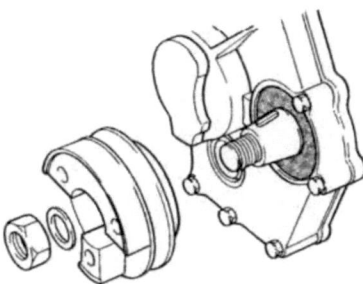

Fig. 66. Fitting of crankshaft pulley

13. Put the key in position in the crankshaft and fit the crankshaft pulley.
    Tightening torque: see Technical data.

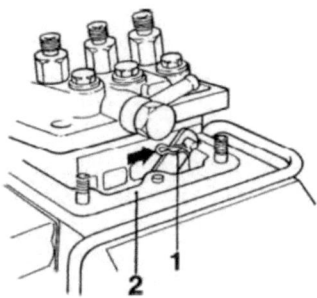

Fig. 65. Fitting of injector pump
1. Lock pin   2. Shims

9. Turn the stop lever clockwise and connect the arm to the injection pump. Fit the lock pin.

Engine body

14. Fit the sea water pump on the timing gear casing. Connect the water hoses to the pump.
15. Fit the drive belt to the alternator.

    Note: If the tension is correct the belt should be able to be pressed in approx. 10 mm (.40 in) between the pulleys.
16. Open the fuel cocks. Bleed the fuel system as per the directions on page 59.
17. Connect the battery leads.

6. MD2010, MD2020: Remove the gear for the mechanical tachometer drive*.

* Note: Mechanical tachometer driving is not used by Volvo Penta. The gear must, however, be in position.

Inspection of valve lifter and camshaft

NOTE! If the lifter is worn over the lift surface the lifter must be scrapped. The "dike" shows that the lifter has not rotated. A dark stripe on the outer lift surface shows, however, that the surface is not worn.

It is the condition of the valve lifters that determines whether further checking of camshaft wear is necessary.

The cam for example may be skew worn in an axial direction. This can in less severe cases be adjusted by grinding the cams. Replace the camshaft in the event of further damage or wear.

Note: When replacing the camshaft all the valve lifters must be replaced.

Camshaft

Dismantling the camshaft

1. Dismantle the cylinder head. See "Dismantling of cylinder head" on page 25. Lift out the valve lifters and place them in order in a rack.
2. Remove the timing gear casing. See under heading "Dismantling of timing gear" on pages 40 and 41.
3. Remove the regulator sleeve from the camshaft.

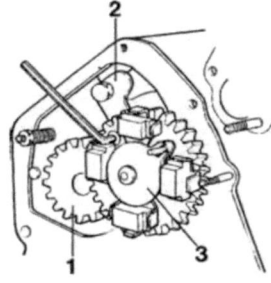

Fig. 67. Dismantling of camshaft
1. Gear
2. Lock washer
3. Regulator sleeve

4. Remove the screws for the lock plate (one screw is accessible through the hole in the camshaft gear), Fig. 67.
5. Lift out the camshaft complete with gear and regulator weights.

   Note: Observe care so that bearings, bearing races or cams are not damaged.

   On MD2030 and MD2040 the gear for the mechanical tachometer drive* must be removed together with the camshaft.

Measuring the camshaft

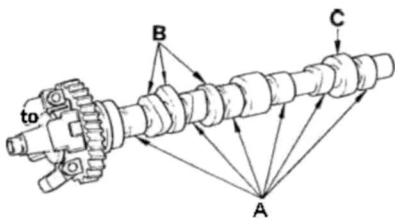

Fig. 68. Measuring the camshaft.

Cam height (inlet and outlet) "A", Fig. 68.
  MD2010, MD2020, MD2030:   min. 26.1 mm
                                                    (1.027 in)
  MD2040:   33.7 mm (1.326 in)

Cam height "B" (for injection pump)
  MD2010, MD2020:   min. 34.3 mm (1.350 in)
  MD2030:   33.8 mm (1.330 in)
  MD2040:   41.8 mm (1.645 in)

Cam height "C" (for feed pump)
  MD2010, MD2020, MD2030:   min. 27.0 mm
                                                    (1.062 in)
  MD2040:   30.0 mm (1.181 in)

Replace the camshaft if the wear tolerances are not maintained.

Fitting the camshaft

Note: If parts have been replaced on the camshaft the fitting of these should take place in the order shown in Fig. 69.

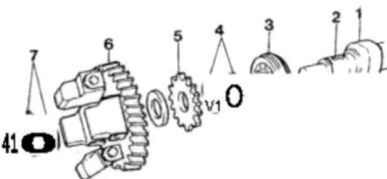

Fig. 69. Camshaft

1. Camshaft
2. Key
3. Roller bearing
4. Spacer rings
5. Gear for drive of mech. tachometer*
6. Camshaft gear
7. Regulator sleeve

* Note: Mechanical tachometers are not used by Volvo Penta, but the gear must still be put in position.

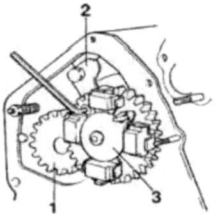

Fig. 70. Fitting the camshaft
1. Gear
2. Lock washer
3. Regulatorsleeve

1. MD2010, MD2020: Fit the gear (1, Fig. 70) for the mechanical tachometer drive*.

2. Oil in the camshaft's bearing races and carefully lift the camshaft in position complete with gear and regulator weights (together with the gear (1) for the mechanical tachometer drive* on MD2030 and MD2040.

   Note: Observe care so that bearings, bearing races or cams are not damaged.

3. Fit the lock washer (2) for the camshaft in the correct position and tighten it. Tightening torque: 9-13 Nm (6.6-9.6 ft.lbs).

4. Fit the regulator sleeve (3). Note: The sleeve should engage with the pin on the camshaft gear.

   * Note: Mechanical tachometers are not used by Volvo Penta, but the gear must still be put in position.

5. Check that the markings on the timing gear correspond (Fig. 58 on page 41).

6. Carry out the work as per items 8 to 11 under the heading "Fitting and adjustment (timing gears) on page 43.

7. Lubricate the mating surface on the valve lifters to the camshaft with molybdenum disulphide and oil in the guides in the cylinder block. Fit the valve lifters in the correct order.

8. Fit the pull rods and rocker mechanism. Tightening torque, see Technical data.

9. Carry out the work as per items 6 to 8 under the heading "Fitting of cylinder head" on page 32.

10. Adjust the valve clearance as per the direction of page 34. Fit the valve cover.

    Tightening torque, see Technical data.

11. Carry out the work as per items 12 to 17 under the heading "Fitting and adjustment (timing gears) on pages 43 and 44.

Engine body

Crank mechanism
Dismantling of crankshaft
(engine removed)

1. Dismantle the reverse gear alt. S-drive and adapter plate and coupling, flywheel and flywheel housing.
2. Remove the cylinder head. See under heading "Dismantling of the cylinder head" on pages 25 and 26.
3. Remove the valve lifters and place them in order in a rack.
4. Remove the pistons with connecting rods. Carry out the work steps to item 5 under the heading "Dismantling of piston, piston rings and connecting rod" on pages 34 and 35.
5. Remove the timing gear casing. Carry out the work steps to item 8 and item 10 under the heading "Dismantling of timing gears" on pages 40 and 41.

Inspection of crankshaft

Clean the crankshaft carefully in all channels after dismantling and inspect it very carefully to confirm whether it really need renovating.

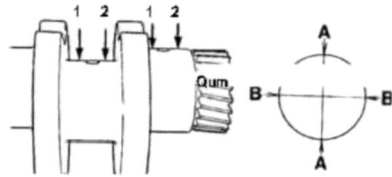

Fig. 72. Check measurement of crankshaft

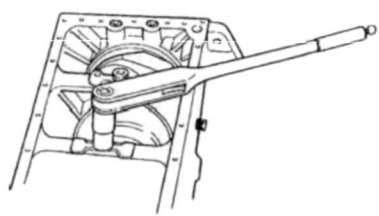

Fig. 71. Dismantling of main bearing cap

6. Remove the lock screws which hold the main bearing cap (Fig. 71). Carefully lift off the crankshaft complete with cap backwards.

   Note: Tape the crankshaft gear to protect the bearing surfaces in the block during dismantling.

1. Check the wear and out-of-roundness with a micrometer. Measure the diameters "A-A" and "B-B" in items "1" and "2" (See Fig. 72).

   The max. permissible conicity and out-of-roundness on the main and big-end bearings is 0.05 mm (.0019 in). Grind the crankshaft to an appropriate undersize if these values are exceeded. Bearing cups are available in two oversizes.

2. Measure the crankshafts longitudinal curvature (distortion). Place the crankshaft on a pair of V-blocks placed under the front and rear of the main bearing journal. Alternatively the shaft can be braced between spikes. Measuring should be carried out on the middle main bearing journal(s).

   Max. longitudinal curvature (distortion): 0.06 mm (.0023 in).

   If this value is exceeded the crankshaft must be aligned or replaced.

3. Check that the mating surfaces on crankshaft seals are not worn or damaged.

7. Remove the main bearing cap from the crankshaft.
   MD2040: Take care of both thrust washers in the rear cap.

Engine body

Grinding of the crankshaft

To achieve satisfactory results in connection with grinding the following factors should be taken into consideration:

1. Grind the crankshaft in a crankshaft grinding machine to the undersize as per "Technical data". Surface fineness 1.6 Z (▽▽▼) for bearing races (B, Fig. 73) and recess radius are achieved by rubbing with emery cloth No. 400.

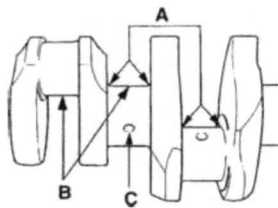

Fig. 73. Checking of recess radius

2. It is very important that the recess radius is the correct size.

   Recess radius:
   - At main and big-end bearing journals, "A" = 3 ± 0.25 mm (.1181 ±.0098 in)
   - At oil holes, "C" = min. 2 mm (.0787 in), max. 5 mm (.1968 in).

   Grinding hacks and sharp edges must be avoided since these can give rise to crankshaft fracture.
3. Clean the crankshaft well from grinding residue and other impurities. Flush and clean the oil channels.

Inspection of front crankshaft bushing

Check the bearing clearance between the big-end journal and bushing. Use a cylinder indicator and a micrometer.

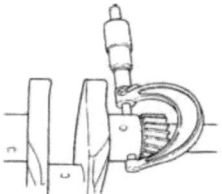

Fig. 74. Checking of bearing clearance

1. Measure the bushing's inner diameter at points 1 and 2 as per Fig. 72 on page 46. Measure in two directions ("A" and "B") at each point.

2. Measure the bearing journal's outer diameter and calculate the bearing clearance (difference between the previous measurement and the bearing journal's max. diameter).

   Max. bearing clearance: 0.2 mm (.0078 in).

Replace the bushing if the clearance exceeds the permissible value. Where necessary the crankshaft can be ground to an appropriate undersize and the bushing can be replaced with a corresponding oversize.

Note: Check the bearing clearance again before the crankshaft is fitted if it has been re-ground.

Inspection of main and big-end bearings

Check the main and big-end bearing cups and the front crankshaft busing. Replace worn bearings or those with damaged bearing surfaces.

Engine body

Replacement of front crankshaft bushing

1. Dismantle the bushing from the cylinder block.
2. Check that the bushing's mating surface in the block has no burrs or upset ends.

5. Check that the oil channel is open after pressing in. Check also the bushing's inner diameter. See "Technical data" for size.

Checking of big-end bearing clearance

Special tool: 856927-9 (measuring plastic)

The big-end bearing's radial bearing clearance can be checked by means of the measuring plastic (part. No. 856927-9) as follows:

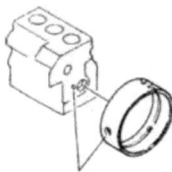

Fig. 75. Marking up of oil hole

3. Draw a line over the hole in the block and bushing with a marker pen (Fig. 75). Oil in the outside of the bushing and its mating surface in the block.

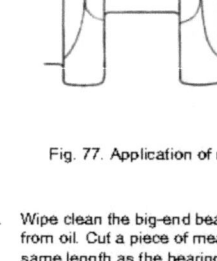

Fig. 77. Application of measuring plastic

1. Wipe clean the big-end bearing and big-end journal from oil. Cut a piece of measuring plastic to the same length as the bearing width and apply the measuring plastic along the big-end journal (Fig. 77).

   Note: Avoid the oil hole.

Fig. 76. Fitting of the bushing

4. Make sure that the bushing's oil hole corresponds with the oil channel in the cylinder block and press in the new bushing to the correct depth.

   NOTE! The bushing should be pressed in from the front of the block and with the bevelled side of the bushing turned forwards (Fig. 76).

2. Fit the connecting rod and cap (note markings correspond) and tighten the crankshaft screws.

   Tightening torque, see Technical data.

   NOTE! Do not turn the connecting rod or crankshaft since this will destroy the measuring strip.

Engine body

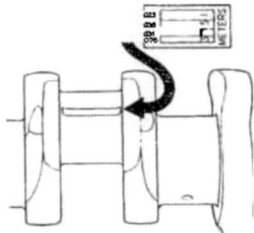

Fig. 78. Check measuring of measuring plastic

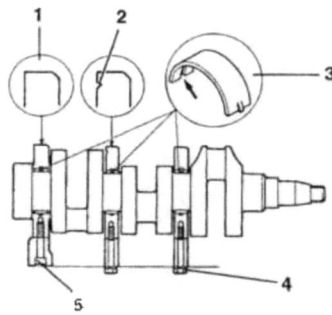

Fig. 79a. Fitting of main bearing cap MD2010, MD2020, MD2030
1. Big-end bearing cap with bevelling
2. Groove
3. Top main bearing half with oil groove
4. Main bearing cap of cast iron
5. Main bearing cap of aluminium

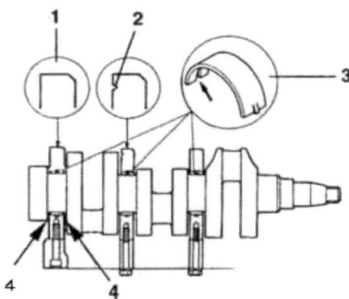

Fig. 79b. Fitting of main bearing cap MD2040
1. Big-end bearing cap with bevelling
2. Groove
3. Top main bearing half with oil groove
4. Thrust washers

3. Remove the cap and measure the width on the pressed out measuring plastic at the widest point. Use the scale which accompanies the measuring plastic (Fig. 78).

   Max. permissible big-end bearing clearance: 0.2 mm (.0078 in).

   Replace the big-end bearing if the bearing clearance exceeds the permissible value. If necessary the journals can be ground to an undersize and oversize bearings fitted. Big-end bearings are available in two oversizes.

   NOTE! Check the bearing clearance again before assembly if the journals have been ground.

Fitting of the crankshaft

1. Check the cleaning of the crankshaft channels and bearing surfaces, cylinder block and cap. Check also that the bearing cups and their mating surfaces have no burrs or upset ends.

2. Place the main bearing in position in the cap.
   Check that the lubrication holes in the top bearing cups come opposite the oil channels.

3. Oil in the bearing and main bearing journals and fit the caps on the crankshaft.

   Note : The bevelled edge (1, Fig. 79a and 79b) should be turned forwards on all caps.

4. Fit the cap which is provided with a groove as per 2, Fig. 79a and 79b.

   Note: The bearing cups provided with an oil groove (3, Fig. 79a and 79b) should be placed in the **top** cap.

   MD2010, MD2020, MD2030: Fit **aluminium** caps (with integrated thrust washers) at the **far end** (flywheel side).

   MD2040: Place both thrust washers in the lower cap at the far end (flywheel side) and with the oil groove turned towards the crankshaft.

5. Carefully lift the crankshaft in position in the cylinder block.

   Note: Tape the crankshaft gear before the crankshaft is lifted in. The cogs can otherwise damage the bearing surfaces in the cylinder block.

Engine body

6. Tighten the main bearing cap. Tightening torque, see Technical data.

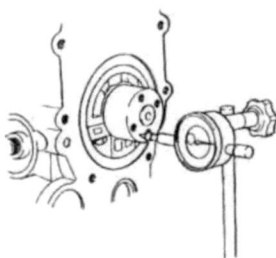

Fig. 80. Checking of axial clearance

7. Check that the axial clearance does not exceed 0.5 mm (.0196 in).

Replacement of gear ring on the flywheel

1. Mark up the position of the flywheel in relation to the crankshaft (to simplify fitting). Dismantle the flywheel.

2. Drill one or a couple of holes in a tooth gap on the gear ring. Split the ring at the drilled hole with a chisel, after which the gear ring can be removed.

3. Brush clean the mating surface on the flywheel with a steel brush.

4. Heat up the new gear ring in an oven (120–150°C/ 248–302°F) so that the gear ring becomes evenly hot all round.

5. Place the heated gear ring on the flywheel and drive on with a hammer and soft mandrel. The gear ring should then cool in the free air.

6. Clean the mating surfaces on the flywheel and crankshaft. Check the rear crankshaft seal. Replace if necessary.

7. Fit the flywheel in the correct position (guide pin on MD2030 and MD2040).

   Tightening torque, see Technical data.

Replacement of rear crankshaft seal

The seal consists of a rubber ring and becomes accessible after the adapter plate at the back of the flywheel housing, the flexible coupling, flywheel* and flywheel housing have been removed.

*Note: Mark up the position of the flywheel in relation to the crankshaft (simplified fitting).

1. Clean the position for the sealing ring in the cylinder block and the mating surface on the flywheel housing.

Fig. 81. Fitting of crankshaft seal

2. Apply an even layer of sealing compound (VP no. 840 879) round the flywheel housing's mating surface (screw holes).
   Apply grease on the sealing lip and fit the seal.

3. Fit the flywheel housing, flywheel, the flexible coupling, and the adapter plate.

   Tightening torque, see Technical data.

Lubricating system

General

The engines are provided with a pressure lubricating system with an oil filter of the full flow type.

Oil pump

The oil pump is placed in the intermediate gear in the transmission, and from where it is also driven.

The pump is of the rotor type with an inner and outer rotor placed eccentrically in relation to each other. The inner rotor has one "cog" less that the outer rotor.

The function of the pump is based on the increase and decrease of the space between the outer and inner rotor cogs. During the first part of the inner rotor's rotation speed the volume is increased, whereby an underpressure occurs and oil is induced in through the inlet. After approx. 1/2 turn the space is reduced and a pressure condition occurs which presses out oil through the outlet.

Reducing valve

The oil pressure is limited by a reducing valve. The valve is placed in the lubricating system just in front of the oil filter and is fitted on the right-hand side of the cylinder block in front of the oil filter.

The valve opens at excessive high pressure and releases oil back to the sump.

Crankcase ventilation

To prevent overpressure and to separate fuel vapour, steam and other gaseous combustion products, the engine is fitted with enclosed crankcase ventilation.

Oil filter

The oil filter is of the full flow type which implies that all the oil is filtered before it is pressed out to the bearing areas.

The filter is placed on the right-hand side of the cylinder block. The filter element consists of folded filter paper.

In the bottom of the filter there is an overflow valve (A, Fig. 82) which opens and releases oil past the filter if the insert should be blocked.

The filter is of the disposable type and is scrapped after use.

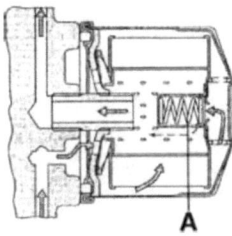

Fig. 82. Oil filter

A. Overflow valve

Lubrication system

Repair instructions

Checking of the oil pressure

The oil pressure can be checked by connecting a manometer with hose to the connection for the oil pressure contact (thread size in cylinder head = 1/8"). The oil pressure should at running speed and temperature be 150-500 kPa (1.5-5 kp/cm^2, 21.3-71.1 lbf/in^2).

If the oil pressure is too high or too low the reducing valve can be replaced first and then the oil pressure checked again.

The valve is fitted on the right-hand side of the cylinder block in front of the oil filter (Fig. 83).

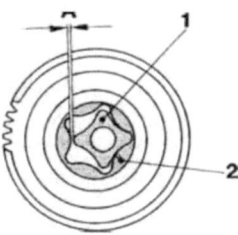

Fig. 84. Checking of oil pump clearance
1. Inner rotor 2. Outer rotor
A. Max 0.25 mm (.0098 in)

Fitting of the oil pump

When fitting the oil pump follow the items 4-10 and 12-17 under the heading "Fitting and adjustment" (transmission) on pages 42-44.

Replacing the oil filter

 WARNING! Hot oil can result in burn injuries.

1. Place a collection vessel under the oil filter.
2. Unscrew the oil filter and discard (watch out for oil spillage). Use a filter extractor.
3. Moisten the new filter's rubber gasket with oil and check its mating surface on the bracket.
4. Screw on the new filter by hand until the gasket makes contact with the sealing surface, and then tighten the filter an additional 1/2 turn.
5. Replenish if necessary the oil in the engine and start it. Check that no leakage occurs.

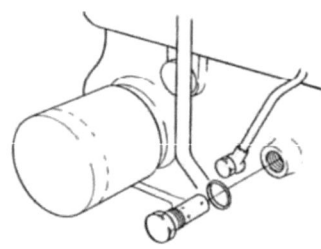

Fig. 83. Replacement of reducing valve

Oil pump

Dismantling of the oil pump

1. See under the heading "Dismantling of the timing gears" on pages 40 and 41. Carry out the work steps 1 to 9.
2. Remove the circlip for the intermediate gear. Take care of the circlip, sleeve washer, spring, shims and oil pump cover.

Oil channels

Clean up and flush the oil channels in the engine with cleaning liquid and then with steam or flushing oil at a pressure of 300-400 kPa (3-4 kp/cm^2, 42.6-56.8 lbf/int) in connection with more extensive engine overhaul.

Note: Do not forget to clean the oil pressure pipe between the cylinder block and cylinder head.

Clean the drilled oil channels in the cylinder block, crankshaft and in the connecting rods with a cleaning brush.

Inspection of the oil pump

1. Check that the oil pump cover and the inner and outer rotor are not worn or damaged.
2. Check the clearance between the outer and inner rotor (Fig. 84). Max. permissible clearance 0.25 mm (.0098 in).

Note. Contact Volvo Penta service department if the shaft journal for the intermediate gear and oil pump needs to be replaced.

Fuel system

General

The fuel is induced by the feed pump from the fuel tank through a water separating pre-filter (accessory) and pressed through the fine filter to the injection pump (Fig. 85).

Return fuel from the injectors is led through the fuel leak pipe/return pipe back to the tank.

Fig. 85. Fuel system, principle drawing

1. Fuel tank
2. Pre-filter
3. Feed pump
4. Fine fuel filter
5. Injection pump
6. Injector

Injection pump

The injection pump is a flange-mounted in-line pump placed on the right-hand side of the engine. The pump is driven via cams on the engine's camshaft which directly activate the pump element.

Centrifugal regulator

The regulator is mechanical and works with speed sensing regulator weights. It is fitted at the front on the camshaft gear from where it is also driven.

The regulator weights activate the injection pump's control rod via the regulator sleeve, a lever and a regulator arm. The speed is regulated over the entire engine speed range, from low idling speed to high speed (universal type).

Feed pump

The feed pump is also positioned on the right-hand side of the engine and is driven via a cam on the engine's camshaft.

Injectors

The engines are fitted with injectors (Fig. 86). Each injector basically consists of a nozzle holder and a nozzle.

When the fuel pressure has increased to the set value (opening pressure) the nozzle needle (pin) (5) lifts which is held pressed against its seat by the thrust washer (6) and atomised fuel is injected into the engine's precombustion chamber.

The injector's opening pressure is determined by the tension of the thrust washer, which in turn is adjusted with adjuster washers (7).

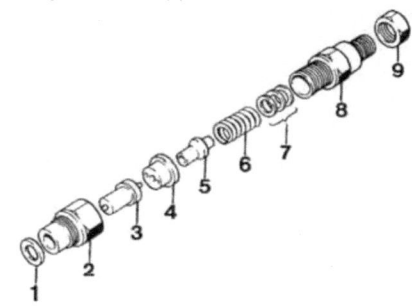

Fig. 86. Injector, complete

1. Packing
2. Nozzle nut
3. Nozzle sleeve
4. Spacer
5. Nozzle needle (pin)
6. Thrust washer
7. Adjuster washers
8. Nozzle holder
9. Nut

Fuel filter

The fuel filter is of the disposable type. The filter insert consists of a specially wound paper filter.

Fuel system

Repair instructions

Observe the greatest possible cleanliness when working with the fuel system.

Injection pump

Dismantling of the injection pump

NOTE! Repair work on the injection pump which may change its setting should only be carried out by specially trained mechanics which have the requisite equipment at their disposal.

Engine warranties are not longer valid if the seals are broken by unauthorised personnel.

1. Carefully wash clean the injection pump, pipes and the engine around the pump.
2. Close the fuel cocks. Remove the delivery pipe complete. Release the fuel hose from the pump.

   Fit protective caps on all connections.

4. Send the pump to an authorised diesel workshop* for inspection if the workshop does not have specially trained personnel with the necessary testing equipment.

   *MD2o10, MD2020, MD2030: Nippondenso.
   MD2040: Bosch.

Fitting of the injection pump

Check that the pump is in good condition, and if so required also tested and approved before it is fitted.

Note: Do not remove the protective caps before the pipes are connected.

1. Put the injection pump in the cylinder block.

   NOTE! Make sure that the shims which were placed under the injection pump flange are put back in place before the pump is put in the block.

   Note: The correct pump setting is normally obtained with this method. If the injection pump, camshaft or cylinder block have been replaced the setting of the pump must be adjusted. See next section, "Adjustment of injection angle".

2. Turn the stop lever clockwise and connect the regulator arm to the control rod on the pump. Fit the lock pin (Fig. 87). Screw tight the pump.
3. Connect the fuel hose and fuel leak pipe to the pump. Fit the delivery pipe.
4. Bleed the fuel system and test run the engine.

Fig. 87. Dismantling of the injection pump
1. Lock pin   2. Shims

3. Dismantle the pump's attachment screws and nuts. Turn the stop lever clockwise and carefully lift up the pump so that the lock pin to the regulator arm becomes accessible (Fig. 87).

   Remove the lock pin and release the regulator arm.

   NOTE! Take care of the shims under the injection pump flange when the pump is lifted off the cylinder block.

Fuel system

Adjustment of injection angle

Fit the injection pump as per the previous section with the exception of item 1 which is changed to item 1 below.

1. Place a shim 0.5 mm (.0196 in) in thickness under the injection pump flange.

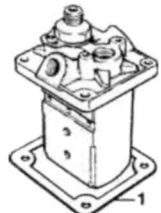

Fig. 88. Fitting of shim
1. Shim

2. Remove the front pressure valve holder from the injection pump.

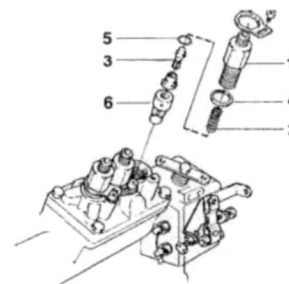

Fig. 89.
1. Pressure valve holder
2. Spring
3. Pressure valve
4. O-ring
5. Copperwasher
6. Pump element

3. Remove the pressure valve and replace the pressure valve holder.

4. Move the throttle arm to max. position. Turn the crankshaft clockwise until the piston in cylinder No. 1 moves upwards in the compression stoke and fuel begins to flow out from the pressure valve (position X in the table below). The work is simplified if an approx. 50 mm (2 in) "observation tube" is fitted on the pressure valve.

Use a scrapped fuel pipe. The pipe makes it easier to see when the fuel begins and stops flowing out from the valve.

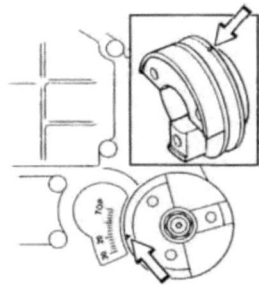

Fig. 90. Marking the pulley and engine block

5. Continue turning the crankshaft slowly clockwise until the fuel stops flowing out from the pressure valve holder. Check the position of the crankshaft to the marking on the pulley and engine block at this point. See Fig. 90.

If the position is after "Y°" (B.T.D.C.) a thinner shims should be used under the injection pump flange. If the position exceeds "Z°" (B.T.D.C.) a thicker shims should be fitted instead. (See table below).

Engine model	Pos. of crankshaft in °			Injection start, crankshaft pos.
	X	Y	Z	
MD2010	30,0	24,5	26,5	24,5-26,5° f.o.d.
M D2020 up to 5101311299	30,0	24,5	26,5	24,5-26,5° B.T.D.C.
from 5101311300	30,0	26,0	28,0	26,0-28,0° B.T.D.C.
M D2030 up to 510101938	30,0	21,5	23,5	21,5-23,5° B.T.D.C.
from * 510101939	30,0	20,5	22,5	20,5-22,5° B.T.D.C.
M D2040A MD2040B **868748	30,0	20,0	22,0	20,0-22,0° B.T.D.C.
MD2040B **868778 MD2040C	30,0	18,0	20,0	18,0-20,0° B.T.D.C.

* engine number - product number

Fuel system

Note: A change of shim size by 0.1 mm (.0039 in) implies that the injection start is moved approx. 1°.

An increase in shim size reduces the injection angle and conversely a decrease in shim size increases the angle.

Shims are available in the following sizes: 0.2, 0.3, 0.4 and 0.5 mm (.0078, .0118, .0157 and .0196 in).

NOTE! In the event that no shims are required, liquid sealing compound should be used.

Replace the pressure valve. Screw in the pressure valve holder by hand. If the pressure valve holder will not go in, screw the holder backwards and forwards quickly 1/4–1/2 turn until the pressure valve goes in the pressure valve holder. Screw down the pressure valve fully by hand until the 0-ring begins to be pressed together. Tighten after this with a 17 mm spanner.

Tightening torque, see Technical data.

Q WARNING! The pressure valve holder must be screwed in by hand so that it is possible to feel that the pressure valve goes correctly into the valve holder. Never use force to screw the valve holder down since this can damage the pressure valve. If the pressure valve cannot be turned in the valve holder the pump must be dismantled and the same method applied with the pump in a completely horizontal position.

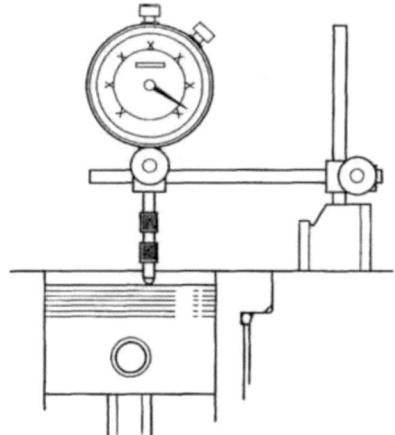

Fig. 91. Measurement of piston position with dial gauge

6. Adjustment of the injection angle can also be made by measuring the piston height with a dial gauge.

The table shows the crankshaft position in degrees when the piston is in a certain position in relation to B.T.D.C.

Carry out the adjustment work as per items 4 and 5.

The table shows the position of the piston in relation to the crankshaft angle ('B.T.D.C.).

Crankshaft angle	MD2010, MD2020 Piston pos.	MD2030 Piston pos.	MD2040 Piston pos.
18° B.T.D.C.	–	2.317 mm	2.875 mm
19° B.T.D.C.	–	2.577 mm	3.199 mm
20° B.T.D.C.	–	2.851 mm	3.539 mm
21° B.T.D.C.	–	3.138 mm	3.895 mm
22° B.T.D.C.	–	3.438 mm	4.267 mm
23° B.T.D.C.	–	3.750 mm	4.655 mm
24° B.T.D.C.	3.636 mm	4.075 mm	5.058 mm
25° B.T.D.C.	3.937 mm	4.413 mm	5.477 mm
26° B.T.D.C.	4.250 mm	4.763 mm	5.912 mm
27° B.T.D.C.	4.573 mm	5.125 mm	–

Crankshaft angle	MD2010, MD2020 Piston pos.	MD2030 Piston pos.	MD2040 Piston pos.
18° BT.D.C.	–	.0912 in.	.1131 in.
19° BT.D.C.	–	.1014 in.	.1259 in.
20° BT.D.C.	–	.1122 in.	.1393 in.
21° BT.D.C.	–	.1235 in.	.1533 in.
22° BT.D.C.	–	.1353 in.	.1679 in.
23° BT.D.C.	–	.1476 in.	.1832 in.
24° BT.D.C.	.1431 in.	.1604 in.	.1991 in.
25° BT.D.C.	.1550 in.	.1737 in.	.2156 in.
26° BT.D.C.	.1673 in.	.1875 in.	.2327 in.
27° BT.D.C.	.1800 in.	.2017 in.	–

Fuel *system*

Setting engine speed (RPM)

Check that the throttle mechanism functions normally. Check that the throttle arm (1) (Fig. moves towards low idle (2) when the throttle mechanism is in idling position and moves towards the stop screw at wide open throttle (WOT) (3) when the throttle mechanism is at wide open throttle (WOT). Adjust the throttle mechanism if necessary. Also check that the air filter and air intake are not blocked.

IMPORTANT! The engine speed (RPM) and fuel quantity are factory set to give maximum output and minimum environmental impact. These settings must not be changed

Seals on the fuel injection pump may only be broken by authorised personnel. Broken seals must always be resealed

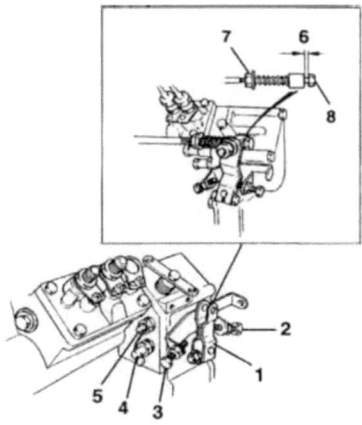

Fig. 92. Setting engine speed (RPM)
1. Throttle arm
2. Adjustment screw, low idling speed
3. Stop screw, wide open throttle (WOT)
4. Adjustment screw, engine racing
5. Adjustment screw, maximum quantity of fuel

Low idle speed

1. Check that gap (6) (Fig. 92) is approximately 3 mm when the throttle mechanism is in the idling position. If necessary: Slacken off the locknut (7) and adjust until the correct gap is obtained with the screw (8).

2. Warm up the engine and check the idling speed using a workshop tachometer (see Technical Data for correct idling speed).

3. If necessary, adjust to the correct idling speed using the adjustment screw (2).

4. Check gap (3) again according to point 1.

Engine racing (high idling speed)

Warm up the engine and check the engine racing speed using a workshop tachometer when the engine has no load at wide open throttle (WOT) (see Technical Data for correct engine racing speed).

Adjust if necessary as follows:

1. Slacken off the stop screw (3) so that it does not limit the movement of the throttle arm (1).

2. Run the engine with no load at wide open throttle (WOT) and adjust to the correct rev speed using the adjustment screw (4) (remember to reseal the screw).

3. Adjust the stop screw (3) so that there is a clearance of 0.1 mm between the stop screw (3) and the throttle arm (1) when the throttle mechanism is at wide open throttle (WOT).

Feed pump

Dismantling of feed pump

1. Wash clean round the pump.

2. Close the fuel cocks. Release the fuel connections from the pump.

3. Dismantle the feed pump from the cylinder block. Empty the pump of fuel.

Fuel system

Injectors

Replacement of injectors

1. Wash clean round the injectors.
2. Release the delivery pipes at the injection pump and at the injectors. Lift off the delivery pipes together.
3. Remove the nut on the top of each injector and lift off the fuel leak pipe.
4. Unscrew the injectors. Use socket, L = 80 mm.

   Socket width = 22 mm (MD2010, 2020, 2040), socket width = 27 mm (MD2030)

   Remove the copper packings under the injectors.

   MD2030: Remove the heat shields (3, Fig. 102).
   MD2010, MD2020, MD2030: Remove the inserts (4) and the inner copper washers.

5. Fit a protective cap on the pipe connections on the injectors over the nozzle if the injector is not to be fitted immediately.
6. Fit the new injector.

   Tightening torque: see Technical data.

7. Fit the fuel leak pipe.
8. Fit the delivery pipes. Check that they do not come skew, and tighten the nuts.

   Tightening torque: 20-25 Nm (14.7-18.4 ft.lbs).

9. Start the engine and check that no leakage occurs.

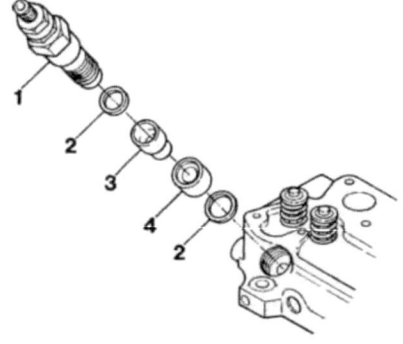

Fig. 102. Dismantling of injector
1. Injector
2. Copper packing
3. Heat shield (MD2030)
4. Insert (MD2010-2030)

Renovating injectors

1. Clean the injector internally.
2. Place the injector (holder) in a vice. Unscrew the nozzle nut and take the injector apart.

   Note: Observe care when taking it apart so that the nozzle needle does not drop out.

3. Pull out the nozzle needle from the nozzle sleeve and place the parts in cleaning petrol.

   Note: Make sure that the nozzle needles and nozzle sleeves which belong together and are adjusted to each other are not mixed up if several nozzles are cleaned together. To avoid confusion the nozzles should be placed in a nozzle rack or in different compartments.

4. Check the nozzle carefully with a lamp magnifier or in a microscope. Check the other parts also.
5. When fitting a **new nozzle** it is important that preserving oil is washed off the nozzle needle and sleeve before the injector is assembled (avoid skin contact with needle's slide surface).

   Clean the parts in pure alcohol. Check that the nozzle needle slides in the sleeve without sticking.

6. Dip the nozzle parts in pure diesel or testing oil and put the injector together. Use the original thickness of adjuster washer(s) to set the opening pressure.
7. Check the opening pressure, jet pattern and tightness in a nozzle testing device.

Fuel system

Testing of injectors

Testing is carried out in a nozzle testing device. The opening pressure and tightness are the most important part of the test. The jet pattern is more difficult to evaluate and does not give a reliable indication of the condition of the nozzle.

 WARNING! Observe care when testing the injectors so that unprotected parts of the body are not hit by the fuel jet from a nozzle. The jet has such a powerful impact that it can penetrate into the skin and cause blood poisoning.

Checking of injectors

Jet pattern

1. Pump with the nozzle testing device and check the jet pattern. The fuel jet should be conformed and in line with the centre line of the nozzle.
2. Check that the fuel jet has a circular cross section.

Tightness

Tightness testing examines potential leakage between the seat of the nozzle needle and the conical sealing surface of the nozzle sleeve.

1. Wipe off the nozzle pin so that it is dry.
2. Pump up the pressure to approx. 2 MPa (20 kp/cm^2, 284.4 lbf/int) under the injector's opening pressure (see Technical data). Hold the pressure constant for 10 seconds and check if any fuel drips from the nozzle pin. Wet nozzles can be approved.

Fit protective caps on the injector's pipe connections and over the nozzle heads if the injectors are not to be fitted immediately.

Adjusting the opening pressure, injector

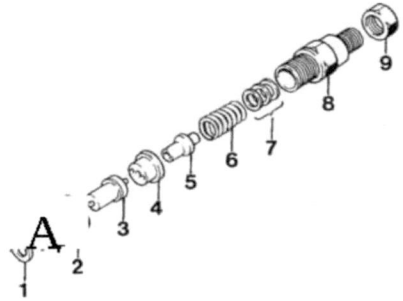

Fig. 103. Adjuster washers (7), injector

Press the nozzle testing device's lever slowly down with the manometer connected until the nozzle opens and releases the fuel. Read off at that precise moment the opening pressure.

If the value read off does not correspond with the prescribed value the setting must be changed. This is done with adjuster washers (Fig. 103).

Note: The opening pressure increases or diminishes with approx. 1 MPa (10 kp/cm^2, 142.2 lbf/int) with a change in the thickness of the adjuster washer by 0.1 mm (.0039 in).

Cooling system

General

The engines are fresh water cooled and fitted with an enclosed cooling system. The system is divided into two circuits.

In the inner circuit (fresh water system) the refrigerant is pumped round by a circulation pump which is driven by a V-belt from the crankshaft pulley.

The fresh water system works at a certain overpressure, whereby the risk of boiling is reduced at high temperatures. A pressure valve opens in the filler cap if the pressure gets higher than normal.

The temperature of the refrigerant is regulated by a thermostat.

The percolation in the sea water system is handled by a gear driven pump of the blade type.

Heat is transferred from the refrigerant to the sea water in a heat exchanger.

As extra equipment the engine can be fitted with a separate expansion tank.

Sea water pump

The sea water pump is fitted on the timing gear housing at the front end of the engine. The pump is driven via the engine's timing gears. The pump wheel (impeller) is manufactured of rubber and is replaceable.

Note: The pump wheel will become damaged if the pump is run dry.

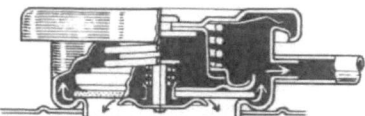

Fig. 104. Filler cap for refrigerant

Thermostat

The engines are provided with a thermostat, the sensor body of which contains wax.

When the engine is cold the thermostat keeps the channel to the heat exchanger closed. The refrigerant then passes via a a by-pass pipe directly back to the induction side of the pump. As the engine heats up the wax increases in volume and the thermostat gradually opens the channel to the heat exchanger, at the same time as the by-pass pipe is closed.

See "Technical data" for opening temperatures.

Repair instructions

NOTE! Close the bottom valve before working on the cooling system.

Refrigerant

The refrigerant has the twin purpose of protecting the cooling system from freezing and preventing corrosion.

Antifreeze

Use a mixture of 50 % Volvo Penta antifreeze (glycol) and 50 % pure water (as neutral as possible). This mixture prevents freezing down to approx. -40° C (-40°F) and should be used all year round.

Note: At least 40 % antifreeze should be used in the system to ensure satisfactory corrosion protection.

Mix the antifreeze with water in a separate vessel before filling the cooling system.

For replenishment of the refrigerant see the instruction on page 64.

WARNING! Antifreeze is hazardous to health (dangerous to consume).

In the event that antifreeze is not necessary it is appropriate to add Volvo Penta anti-corrosion agent 1141526-2.

Draining of the refrigerant

Stop the engine before draining the cooling system.

The fresh water system

1. Unscrew the filler cap. Turn the cap to the first stop and wait a moment before lifting off the cap.

    WARNING! Open the filler cap very carefully if the engine is hot. Steam or hot liquid may spit out.

2. Connect a hose to the drain cock. Open the cock and drain out the refrigerant in a vessel.

    Hand in the mixture to a recovery station if it is not to be used again. Never pollute the water.

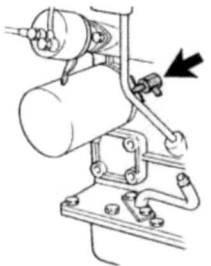

Fig. 105. Draining of the refrigerant

The sea water system

Watch out for the penetration of water in the boat!

1. Close the bottom cock or the cock on the S-drive. Release the cover on the sea water pump and let the water run out.

2. Release the hose from the sea water pump and sea water filter at the reverse gear and tilt down so that the water runs out.

3. Check if there are additional cocks/plugs at low points on the refrigerant and exhaust pipes. Check carefully that all the water runs out.

4. Tighten the hoses and cover to the sea water pump.
    Pump out the boat and check that there is no leakage.

Cooling system

Replenishment of refrigerant

Flush the cooling system before filling up with refrigerant.

Close all the drain points and fill up with refrigerant to the correct level. See next page.

Filling should be done with an idle engine. The engine must not be started before the system is vented and completely filled. If a heater unit is connected to the engine's cooling system the heat control valve must be fully opened and the unit vented during filling.

Check hoses and connections and seal any leaks.

Note: Fill the **system slowly!** Filling should not be done too quickly or else air pockets can form in the system. The air should be allowed to flow out through the filling opening. Check the engine coolant level after running the engine for some time. Top up coolant if required.

MD 2010-2040C
Refrigerant level

Check the engine coolant level

WARNING! Do not open the engine coolant system filler cap when the engine is still hot except in an emergency Steam or hot coolant may spray out.

Turn the filler cap to the first stop and let any pressure escape from the system before removing the cap. Top up coolant if necessary. For MD2010-2040A/B the level must be just under the neck of the filler opening and for MD2010-2040C between the lower edge of the neck of the filler opening and the level spur (1). Reinstall the filler cap.

If a separate expansion tank is installed (optional extra) the level should be between the MAX and MIN marks.

Refrigerant temperature too low

If the refrigerant temperature is too low this may be because of:
- Defective thermostat.
- Defective temperature sensor or instrument.

Refrigerant temperature too high

If the refrigerant temperature is too high this may be because of:

Blocked sea water inlet or sea water filter.

Defective pump wheel in the sea water pump.

Too low refrigerant level, air in the fresh water system.

Slipping or burst belt for the circulation pump.

Defective thermostat, temperature sensor or instrument.

Blocked cooling system.

Incorrectly set injection pump, i.e. injection angle.

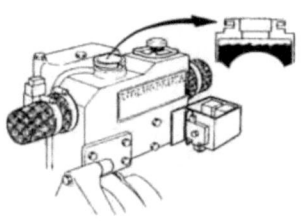

MD 2010-2040A/B
Refrigerant level

Refrigerant loss

There are two types of refrigerant loss:
- Refrigerant loss when running.
- Refrigerant after stopping with a hot engine.

Refrigerant loss when running may be because the cooling system is not tight or because air or combustion gases have been forced into the system.

Cooling system

Checking of pressure valve in filler cap

Special tool: 999 6662

1. Drain off the refrigerant and connect the pressure testing device with a nipple to one of the plugged holes in the cooling system.

2. Extend the drain hose from the filler pipe with a hose the end of which is placed in a vessel containing water.

3. Apply the pressure and read off the manometer when the valve opens (water bubbles in vessel).

   The valve should open at 0.9 kp/cm^2 (12.8 lbf/in^2).

4. Remove the test equipment. Fit the plug and fill up with refrigerant.

Cleaning of heat exchanger

Clean the heat exchanger insert on signs of blocking (slow rise in refrigerant temperature).

NOTE! Check/clean the sea water filter first. Check also the sea water pump's impeller and sea water intake.

Important! Close the bottom valve before working on the cooling system.

1. Drain off the water in the sea and fresh water systems.

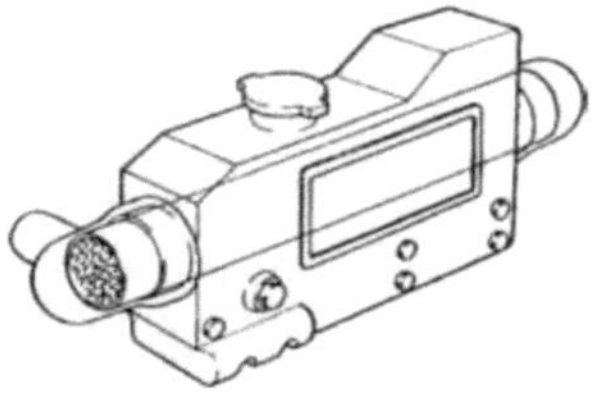

2. Release the hose clips and remove the rubber muffs at the front and back of the heat exchanger. Pull out the insert.

3. Flush and clean the insert inside and outside. Clean also the housing.

   Note: If there are loose deposits in the insert a suitable steel rod can be pushed through the tubes in the opposite direction to the flow of water.

   NOTE! Make sure that the rod does not damage the tubes.

4. Fit the insert in the heat exchanger. **NOTE! Make sure that the insert is positioned correctly.** Make sure that the hole in the insert casing comes opposite the hole in the housing and that the vent hole comes upwards. The insert is marked with "UP".

   Place the insert so that its extruding parts are equal at the front and back.

5. Fit the rubber muffs on the heat exchanger's front and back and tighten the hose clips. Connect the hose from the sea water pump and tighten the clip.

6. Fill up with refrigerant.

7. Open the bottom cock or the cock on the S-drive and start the engine. Check that no leakage occurs.

Fig. 106. Heat exchanger insert

Cooling system

Replacing the circulation pump
Dismantling
1. Drain off the refrigerant from the engine (fresh water system).

2. Release the alternator and remove the drive belt.
   MD2030, MD2040: Remove the clamp for the alternator.

3. Remove the rubber hoses to and from the pump.

4. Release the electric cables to the temperature relay.

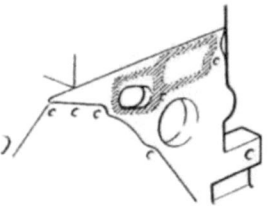

Fig. 108. Application of sealing compound (silicon)

3. Apply sealing compound (silicon, Volvo Penta part No. 1161277-7) on the cylinder block as per Fig. 108, shaded area.
   Fit the refrigerant pump with a new gasket.

4. MD2030, MD2040: Fit the clamp to the alternator.

5. Fit the rubber hoses at the pump's inlet and outlet. Tighten the hose clips.

6. Fit the drive belt. It should be possible to press the belt down approx. 10 mm (.40 in) between the pulleys.

7. Connect the contact piece to the temperature relay.

8. Fill up with refrigerant. Start the engine and check that no leakage occurs.

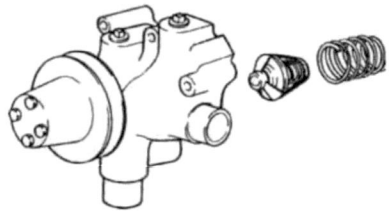

Fig. 107. MD2030. Circulation pump

5. Remove the pump's attachment screws and lift off the pump.
   MD2030: Remove the back piece (plate), spring, and thermostat.

Fitting
1. Clean the mating surfaces on the pump and cylinder block.

2. MD2030: Place the thermostat and spring in the pump. Fit the back piece (plate) on the pump with a new gasket.

Replacing the pump wheel in the sea water pump

Close the bottom cock, or the cock on the S-drive before working on the cooling system.

1. Dismantle the pump's end cover and drain off the water in the sea water system.

Cooling system

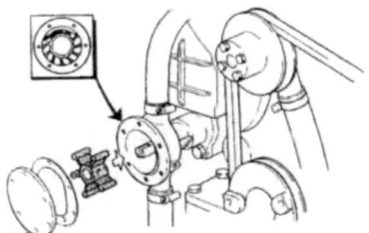

Fig. 109. Replacing the pump wheel

2. Pull and twist out the pump wheel (impeller) with a pair of universal pliers.

3. Clean the housing internally. Grease in the pump housing and inside of the cover with a little grease.

4. Press in the new wheel with a rotational motion (clockwise). Fit the sealing washer on the outer end of the centre of the wheel.

5. Fit the cover together with a new gasket.

6. Open the bottom cock, or the cock on the S-drive. Start the engine and check that no leakage occurs.

Thermostat

Replacing the thermostat

Note: On MD2030 the thermostat is accessible after the circulation pump has been removed. See under heading "Replacing the circulation pump" on page 66.

Other engines:

1. Remove both battery leads. Drain off the water in the fresh water system.

2. MD2010, MD2020: Drain off the water in the sea water system. Remove the alternator.

M D2040   MD2010-2020

M D2030

Fig.110. Positioning of the thermostat
1. Cover

3. MD2010, MD2020: Release the exhaust pipe and remove the heat exchanger housing complete. Remove the spring and lift out the thermostat from the housing.

4. MD2040: Remove the cover (1) on the front left-hand side of the heat exchanger. Remove the rubber ring.

Checking the thermostat

1. Check that the thermostat closes completely.
2. Heat up water in a vessel to 68°C / 154.4°F (MD2010, MD2020), or to 75°C / 167°F (MD2030, MD2040).
3. Submerge the thermostat in the water. Check after at least 3-5 minutes that the thermostat is still closed.
4. Raise the temperature to boiling point (100°C / 212°F). Check after 3-5 minutes that the thermostat has opened at least 6 mm /.02362 in (MD2010, MD2020), or to 8 mm /.3149 in (MD2030, MD2040).

Replace the thermostat if these specifications are not met. NOTE! If the thermostat does not close completely the engine will run at too low a temperature.

Electrical system

General

The engines are fitted with AC generators. The system voltage is 12V.

MD2010A, -2020A, -2030A and -2040A are fitted with a 1,5-pole* electrical system, while MD2010B/C, 2020B/C, 2030B/C and 2040B/C have a one-pole system.

* Note: One-pole during the start procedure via an earthing relay.

The electrical system also includes as accessories relays for the monitoring of the engine's refrigerant temperature and oil pressure.

The electrical system is illustrated in two ways. The wiring diagram (page 80) shows the wiring, cable areas and colours.

Where respective parts are positioned on the engine is shown in the figures below.

Positioning of electrical components on the engine

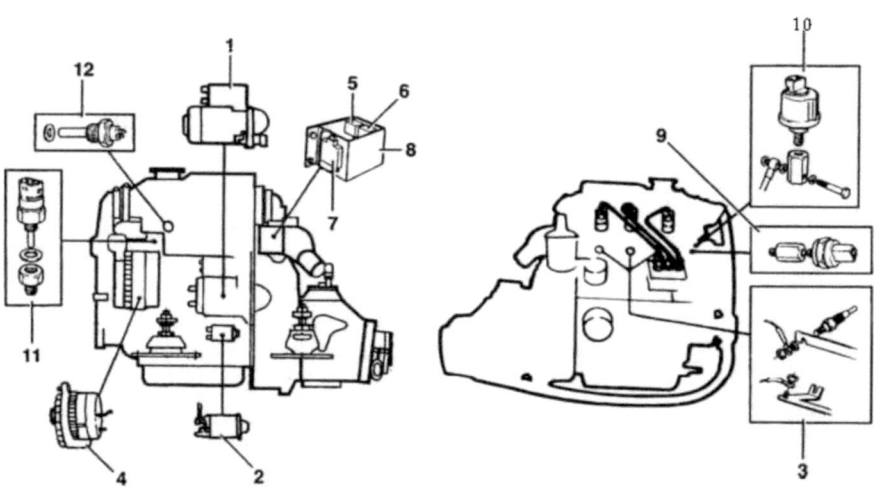

Fig. 111. Positioning of electrical components on the engine

1. Starter motor
2. Earthing relay (A-version)
3. Glow plug
4. Alternator
5. Starter relay
6. Glow relay
7. Fuses (4 pcs), max. 15A (+)
8. Fuses (4 pcs), max. 15A (-) (A-version)
9. Oil pressure relay, (accessory)
10. Oil pressure sensor
11. Refrigerant temperature relay (accessory)
12. Refrigerant temperature sensor

Electrical system

Fuses

The fuses are placed in the relay box at the rear left-hand side of the engine. The fuses disconnect the current when overloaded.

MD2010A, -2020A, -2030A and -2040A are fitted with two fuse blocks each with four fuses (15A) for plus (+) and minus (-).

MD2010B/C, -2020B/C, -2030B/C and -2040B/C have only one fuse block with four fuses (15A) for plus (+).

Re-connect the electrical system, after inspection and work, if one fuse has triggered by moving the cable connection to the next contact.

Relays

The relays are placed in the relay box on the rear left-hand side of the engine.

The start and glow functions are controlled via their own switching relay. These relays are identical and therefore if necessary can be interchanged.

Alternator

Voltage regulator with sensor system

The voltage regulator to the standard alternator (14V/60A) is provided with a sensor system.

The sensor system compares the charge voltage between the alternator's connections B+ and 13- with that between the batteries' plus and minus poles. The voltage regulator then compensates any voltage drop in the cables between alternator and batteries by increasing the charge voltage when necessary from the alternator.

On delivery from Volvo Penta the sensor system is not activated. Connection has, however, in all probability been carried out in connection with the installation of the engine.

Connection of sensor system

Important! Stop the engine and then switch off the current with the main switches before working on the electrical system.

1. Release the yellow sensor conductor from connection B+ on the alternator.
2. Splice the conductor (yellow, 1.5 mm^2, 16 AWG) and connect it to the batteries' plus pole (+).

Charging distributor

As an accessory the engine's standard alternator can be provided with a charging distributor. Two separate battery circuits can thereby be charged simultaneously. The charging distributor separates both groups from each other so that the engine's start battery is maintained fully charged even if the "accessory batteries" are weak or almost flat.

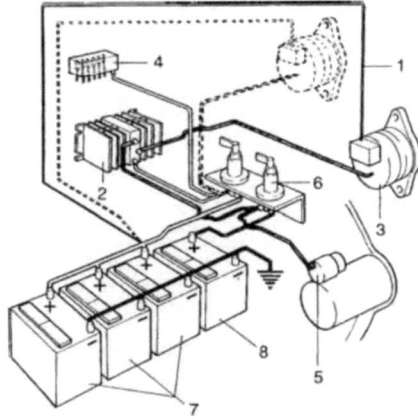

Fig. 112. Connection of sensor system to standard alternator, principle drawing

1. Sensor conductor (yellow, 1.5 mm^2, 16 AWG)
2. Charging distributor (accessory)
3. Alternator
4. Fuse panel (accessory)
5. Starter motor
6. Main switch
7. Accessory batteries (accessory)
8. Start battery (engine)

Electrical system

Important information on the electrical system

A **IMPORTANT!** Stop the engine and switch off the current with the main switch before working on the electrical system.

1. **Main switch**

    Never break the current circuit between the alternator and battery when the engine is running. The main switch must never be switched off before the engine has stopped. If the current is broken while the engine is running the voltage regulator can be destroyed and the alternator seriously damaged.

    For the same reason the charging circuits must not be switched over when the engine is running. For simultaneous charging of two separate battery circuits it is possible to fit a Volvo Penta charging distributor to the standard alternator (accessory).

2. **Batteries**

    Never switch the batteries plus and minus poles when fitting the batteries. This can result in serious damage to the electrical equipments. Compare with the wiring diagram. The battery poles should be well cleaned and the lead lugs always tight and well greased to ensure good contact.

    Quick charging of batteries should be avoided. If quick charging must be used, then both battery leads should always be removed first.

    NOTE! Follow the relevant safety instructions when charging batteries. During charging the cell plugs should be unscrewed but remain in the plug holes. Ventilate well, especially if the batteries are charged in a closed room. Always switch off the charging current **before** the charge clamps are released.

    WARNING! The battery compartment must never be exposed to a naked flame or electrical sparks. Never smoke in the vicinity of batteries. Hydrogen gas develops during charging which when mixed with air forms oxyhydrogen gas. This gas is highly inflammable and very explosive.

    Always use protective goggles when charging and handing batteries.

    The battery electrolyte contains strongly corrosive sulphuric acid. In the event of skin contact, wash with soap and plenty of water. If battery acid gets in your eyes, rinse immediately with plenty of water and contact a doctor immediately.

3. **For starting with auxiliary battery, see instructions of page 71.**

4. **Electric cables**

    Never make holes in the cable insulation to conduct measurements. In a corrosive environment such as in a boat it takes approx. 2 years for thin cables to oxidise off via the hole.

    If a hole must be made in the insulation, it should be sealed with an appropriate glue afterwards.

5. **Connection of extra equipment**

    All extra equipment should be connected to a separate terminal box and be fused. Extra power points directly from instrument panels should be avoided. Permissible extra outlets are a **total of max. 5A** (for all instrument panels together).

Electrical system

Galvanic corrosion

MD2010B/C, MD2020B/C, MD2030B/C, MD2040B/C

The engine's flywheel housing and transmission (reverse gear/S-drive) are electrically insulated from the engine. Note the fitting sequence on the screw union (Fig. 113). The insulation sleeve pos. 1 is only fitted on one of the screws (optional screw).

WARNING! The flywheel housing or transmission (reverse gear alt. S-drive) must under no circumstances be earthed. Earthing of these components can result in serious damage as a result of galvanic corrosion.

Electric welding

Remove the plus and minus leads from the batteries, and then remove all cables to the alternator.

Always connect the welding clip to the component which is to be welded and as close to the weld point as possible. The clip must never be connected to the engine or so that the current can pass over a bearing.

On completion of welding: Always connect the cables to the alternator **before** the battery leads are replaced.

Repair instructions

Starting with auxiliary battery

WARNING! The batteries (especially the auxiliary battery) contain oxyhydrogen gas which is very explosive. A spark, which can occur if the auxiliary battery is incorrectly connected, is sufficient to cause the battery to explode and result in injury.

Note: If the start battery has frozen it must be thawed first before a start attempt is made with the auxiliary battery. Check that the battery is not damaged before connecting it again.

1. Check that the auxiliary battery's rated voltage corresponds to the engine's system voltage (12V).

2. Connect the red auxiliary lead (+) to the auxiliary battery and then to the flat battery. Then connect the black auxiliary lead (-) to the auxiliary battery, and finally to a point **some distance from the flat batteries**, e.g. at the main switch on the minus lead or at the minus lead's connection on the starter motor (2-pole electrical system), or at the minus lead's connection on the engine (one-pole system).

3. Start the engine. **NOTE! Do not touch the connection during the attempt to start (risk for sparks) and do not lean over any of the batteries.**

4. Remove the leads in exactly the reverse order to the way they were connected. **NOTE! The ordinary leads to the standard battery must absolutely not be disconnected.**

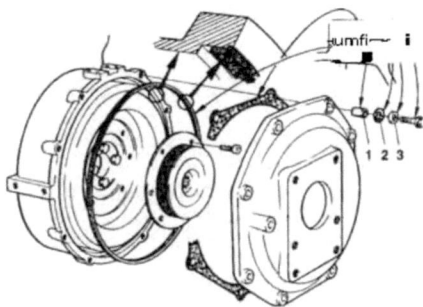

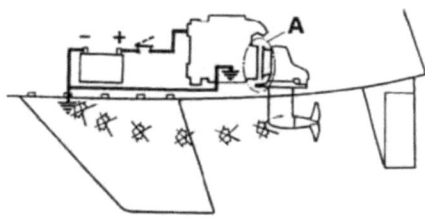

Fig. 113. Electrical insulation (A) of the flywheel housing and transmission

1. Insulation sleeve 2. Insulation washer
3. Washer

Checking the battery leads

Set the multimeter for voltage testing and then connect the multimeter between the battery's plus and minus pole. Run the engine at approx. 2000 rpm. Read off and note the voltage over the battery poles.

The alternator provides approx. 14.0 V:

Conduct test as follows:

Connect the multimeter between the alternator's B+ and B- connections.

Run the engine at approx. 2000 rpm. The alternator should provide 14.0-14.4 V. The total voltage drop must not exceed 0.4 V.

Voltage drop less than 0.2 V:
Battery leads in good condition.

Voltage drop more than 0.3 V:
Conduct check of battery leads.

The alternator provides more than 14.4 V:

See items "Checking and troubleshooting of alternator" and "Checking of the regulator".

Checking of positive battery lead

Connect the multimeter between the alternator's B+ connection and the battery's plus pole.

Run the engine at approx. 2000 rpm. The voltage drop must not exceed 0.2 V. If the voltage drop exceeds this value the lead connections must be rectified as per the "Procedure" below.

After this carry out a test as per "Checking of negative battery charging".

Checking of negative battery lead

Connect the multimeter between the alternator's B- connection and the battery's minus pole (-).

Run the engine at approx. 2000 rpm. The voltage drop must not exceed 0.2 V. If the voltage drop exceeds this value the lead connections must be rectified as per the "Procedure" below.

Procedure

 WARNING! Disconnect the current and remove both battery leads before working on the charging circuit.

If the voltage drop during any of the tests as per the items above exceeds 0.2 V the lead connections must be removed and cleaned from oxide etc. Spray the connections with a moisture repellant contact oil (Volvo Universal oil, part. No. 1161398-1) or the like and tighten the connection again.

Rectify the connections at the battery, main switch, starter motor, alternator, glow relay and glow plug.

Alternator

Checking and troubleshooting of the alternator

Dismantle the alternator's electrical connections.

Spanner widths 8 and 10 mm.

Remove the alternator belt. Dismantle the alternator. Spanner widths 1 1/16"; 5/8", 12 mm and 13 mm.

Release the voltage regulator's connections at the alternator's B+ connection. Remove the flat pin at connection B+ and D+. Remove the cap on the W connection.

Bend the plastic guard's attachment lugs alternately off the alternator. Release the regulator's two connection cables to the diode bridge. Use long-nose pliers or poke out the cable lugs with a screwdriver. Do not pull the cables!

Replacement of carbon brushes in the alternator

Unscrew the voltage regulator. Unscrew the brush holder. Check the length of the carbon brushes. Replace the brushes if they are 5 mm (.1968 in) or shorter. Carbon and holder are replaced as one unit. Unsolder the connection cables and solder on the new ones with an acid-free soft solder.

Electrical system

Checking of the regulator

Special tool: Regulator tester 884892-1

Check before testing that the instrument's batteries have the correct voltage. Press in the button "Test" and check that the green lamp ("Batt.") lights. Replace the batteries (2 pcs alkaline, 9 V) if the lamp does not light.

The batteries are in a compartment underneath the instrument.

Connect the tester's grey cables to the carbon.

Connect the tester's brown cable to the regulator's yellow and brown cables which should be put together during the test.

Connect the tester's black cable to the regulator's black cable.

Press the "Test" button and at the same time turn the rheostat from the "0" marking to the "1" marking.

Regulator in good condition

The red and green lamps should light from "0". The red lamp should go off at the "1" marking.

Faulty regulator

Replace the regulator if the red lamp lights constantly when the rheostat is turned, or if it does not light in any position.

Note: The "2" marking on the tester is not used for this type of regulator.

Check measurement of rotor winding

After the regulator and carbon brushes have been removed it is possible to measure the resistance of the rotor.

Set the measuring instrument in position Ω. Make sure that the probes have good contact between the slip rings. The resistance of the rotor should be 3.0-5.0 Ω.

Check also that no earth fault occurs by measuring between slip ring and earth.

Dismantling the diode bridge

In order to check the diode bridge and stator windings the diode bridge should be dismantled.

Unsolder the three stator windings. Avoid excessive heat since this can damage the diodes. Release the nuts (note how the washers and nuts are fitted).

Check measurement of the diode bridge

Set the multimeter in the position "Diode test". Be very careful to obtain good contact with the probes during all measurements.

Checking of the B+ diodes

Connect the measuring instrument's positive probe to one of the stator winding connections (1-2-3). Connect the instrument's negative probe to the diode plate's B+. Read off the instrument. A normal value should lie between 450 and 650 mV, which is the voltage drop over the diode. An other value indicates a defective diode.

Check the other B+ diodes by moving the positive probe to the respective connection (1-2-3).

Check the B+ diodes in the opposite direction of current flow by switching the position of the positive and negative probes. Carry out the same measurement procedure as above. The instrument should during this measurement show a one "1" (to far left). If the instrument shows another value the diode is defective.

Checking of the B- diodes

Connect the instrument's positive *probe* to the diode plate's B- connection and the instrument's negative *probe* to the respective stator winding connection (1-2-3).

Read off the instrument as before. A normal value should lie between 450 and 650 mV. Another value indicates a defective diode.

Electrical system

Check the 13- diodes in the opposite direction of current flow by switching the position of the positive and negative probes. Carry out the same measurement procedure as above.

The instrument should during this measurement show a one "1" (to far left). If the instrument shows another value the diode is defective.

Note: If any diode is defective the entire diode plate must be replaced.

Checking of the D+ diodes

The diode plate's three magnetising diodes are check according to the same principle as above.

Connect the measuring instrument's positive probe to the respective connection for the stator winding (1-2-3) and the instrument's negative probe to D+. The voltage drop for the respective diode should be between 450 and 650 mV.

Check the D+ diodes in the opposite direction of current flow and switch the positions of the positive and negative probes. Carry out the same measuring procedure as above. The instrument should show a one "1" (to far left). If the instrument shown another value the diode is defective.

Note: If any diode is defective the entire diode plate must be replaced.

Check measurement of the stator windings

When the diode bridge is removed it is possible to measure the stator windings with the multimeter set to the "Buzzer" position.

Measure the resistance between respective windings.

NOTE! Check first the inner resistance in the measuring cables. When the measurement between the stator windings is carried out the measuring cable's inner resistance (e.g. 0.10 Ω) must be deducted from the value obtained.

Measure between all winding connections (three measurements). The resistance should lie at 0.10 S2.

Measure also against the alternator material by connecting the instrument in position S2. Measure between the respective winding and the material. The instrument should during this measurement show a one "1" (which implies infinite).

If the instrument shows another value the stator winding is defective.

Note: If any stator winding is defective the stator must be replaced as a complete unit.

Starter motor
General

The stator motor is a DC series motor. The starter gear is controlled by a magnet and is moveable in an axial direction on the rotor shaft.

On engine MD2040 the starter motor is provided with a reduction gear. This enables a higher torque.

Electrical system

Dismantling of the starter motor

1. Remove both battery leads.
2. Release the electric cables to the starter motor.
3. Dismantle the starter motor's attachment screws and lift off the starter motor.

Stripping of the starter motor

1. Clean the exterior of the starter motor.

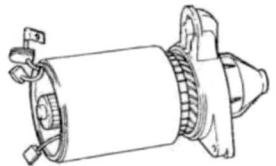

Fig. 117. Dismantling of the stator housing

5. Remove the brush holder plate. Remove the stator housing from the rotor and front bearing shield; on 2040 from the gear housing.

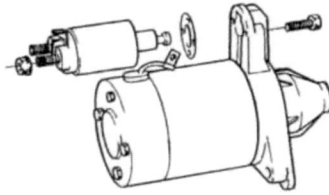

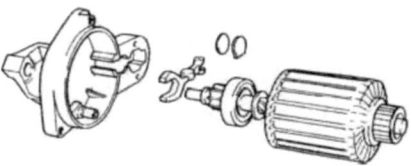

Fig. 115. Stripping of the starter motor

Fig. 118. Dismantling of the rotor

2. Remove the magnet.

3. Remove the protective cover from the rear bearing shield. Remove the lock ring and where appropriate the intermediate washer(s).

6. Remove the coupling arm and rotor.

   MD2040: The coupling arm is fitted in the gear housing.

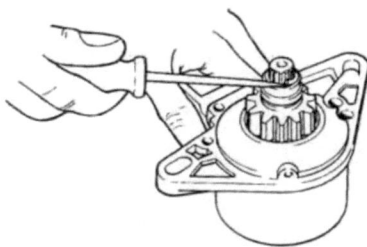

Fig. 119. Dismantling of the starter gear

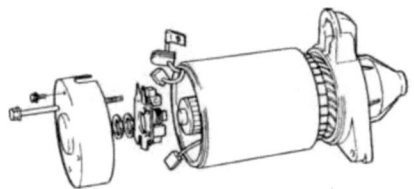

7. Remove the starter gear as per Fig. 119. First remove the lock ring by tapping down the contact ring with a suitable mandrel.

   MD2040: The starter gear is fitted in the gear housing.

Fig. 116. Dismantling of the bearing shield

4. Remove the rear bearing shield.

Inspection of the starter motor

Troubleshooting on the starter motor should be handed over to an authorised electrical workshop which disposes over the necessary test equipment.

1. Test the rotor with respect to winding flash-over and failure with the test equipment for this purpose.

Fig. 120. Checking of the commutator

2. Check that the mating surfaces for the electric brushes on the commutator are smooth and free from dirt and oil. If the commutator is damaged or burnt it can be polished with sandpaper No. 500 or 600.

   Measure the commutator with a dial gauge. Max. permissible radial distortion is 0.05 mm (.0019 in).

3. Check that the commutator's insulation lies at least 0.2 mm (.0078 in) below the laminated surface. Correct if necessary. See Fig. 120.

4. Check the linearity of the rotor. Brace the rotor between spikes and measure the radial distortion on the rotor frame with a dial gauge. Max. permissible radial distortion is 0.08 mm (.0031 in).

   Note: The radial distortion is half of the read value.

5. Check the cogs on the starter gear. Replace damaged gear. Check also the starter gear ring if the gear is damaged.

Field winding

Check with a test instrument that there is no failure in the winding. If the field winding is defective it should be replaced.

Assembly of the starter motor

Assembly is carried out in the reverse order to stripping.

Connect + and - from a 12 V battery to the terminal on the magnet and check that the starter gear is pushed forward to the gear stop.

Fitting of the starter motor

1. Place the starter motor in position in the flywheel housing and tighten it.
2. Connect the electric cables to the starter motor. See the wiring diagram on page 80-86.
3. Connect both battery leads.

Electrical components

Relay box with fuses

The A-version has two fuse blocks each with four fuses (15A) for plus (+) and minus (-) placed on the relay box at left-hand rear side of the engine.

The B/C-version has one fuse block.

The fuses disconnect the current in the event of overloading.

Re-connect the electrical system of a fuse has blown by moving the cable connection to the next contact.

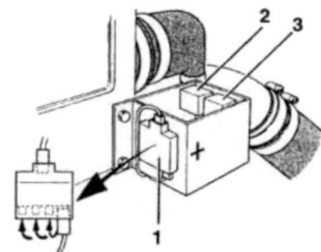

Fig. 121. Relay box with fuses
1. Fuse block + (15A)
2. Starter relay
3. Glow relay

Electrical system

Relays

Oil pressure relay - alarm

Fig. 122. Oil pressure relay

Contact type: Normally open. The contacts close if the oil pressure in the engine drops below 0.3 ± 0.15 bar (4.18 ± 2 psi).

Note: Checking of the closing point should be conducted with **falling** pressure.

Refrigerant temperature relay - alarm

Fig. 124. Refrigerant temperature relay

Contact type: Normally open. The contact closes if the refrigerant temperature rises over 95°C ± 3°C (203°F ± 5.6°F).

Note: Checking of the break point should be conducting with **rising** temperature.

Sensors

Note: Sensors are only available with "De Luxe" instrument panels.

Oil pressure sensor

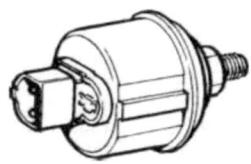

Fig. 125. Oil pressure sensor

Resistance testing: Measure with falling pressure and with instrument connected. Measure with ohmmeter class 1 at +20° C (+68°F)

Pressure		
0 bar (0:		10 +3 /-5 Ω
2 bar (27.9 psi):		52 ±4 Ω
4 bar (55.8 psi):		88 ± 4 Ω
6 bar (83.7 psi):		124 ±5 Ω

Refrigerant temperature sensor

Fig. 126. Refrigerant temperature sensor

Resistance sensor: Measure with the sensor submerged to the hexagonal screw for three minutes in circulating liquid and with the current switched on.

Temp.		
60°C (+140°F):	134.0 ±13.5 Ω	(t4°C, t7.2°F)
90°C (+194°F):	51.2 ±4.3 Ω	(t4°C, ±7.2°F)
100°C (+212°F):	38.5 ±3.0 Ω	(t40C, t7.20F)

Engine MD2010A, MD2020A, MD2030A, MD2040A

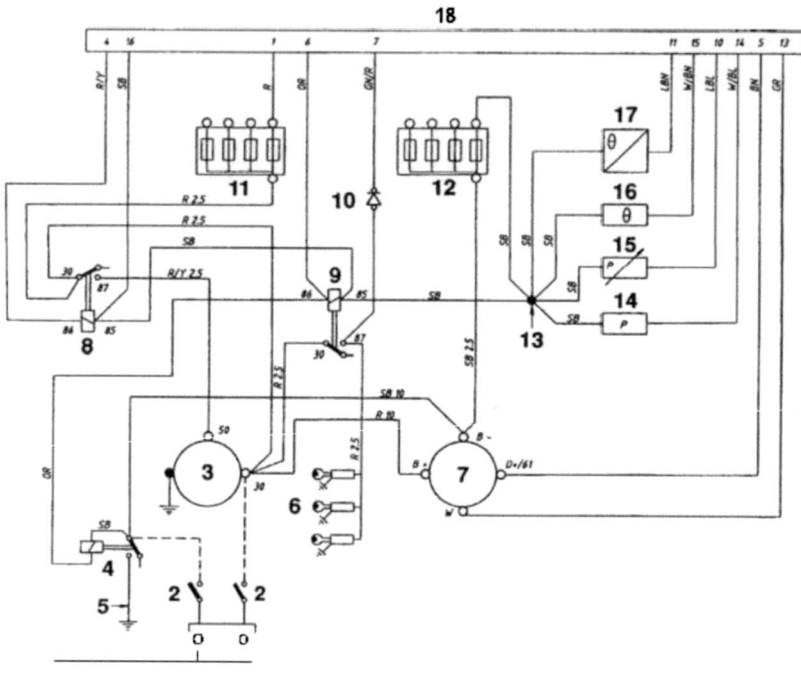

1. Battery
2. Main switch
3. Startermotor
4. Earthing relay
5. Earth rail
6. Glow plug*
7. Alternator
8. Starter relay
9. Glow relay
10. Protective diode
11. Fuses (4 pcs), max. 15A (+)
12. Fuses (4 pcs), max. 15A (-)
13. Splice
14. Oil pressure relay, engine (normally open, closed at 0.3 bar ±0.1 bar
15. Oil pressure sensor
16. Refrigerant temperature relay (normally open, closes at 95°C ±3°C, 203,2 °F±5.6°F)
17. Refrigerant temperature sensor
18. Connector, 16-pole

* MD2010: 2 pcs. Other engines: 3 pcs

Cable colours

BL =	Blue	OR	Orange
LBL =	Light blue	R	Red
BN =	Brown	SB	Black
LBN =	Light brown	W	White
GN =	Green	Y	Yellow
GR =	Grey		

Cable areas in mm² are given after the colour code in the wiring diagram.
Areas not given = 1.0 mm².
Dashed cables are not included from Volvo Penta.

Wiring diagram

Engine MD201OB/C, MD202OB/C, MD203OB/C, MD204OB/C

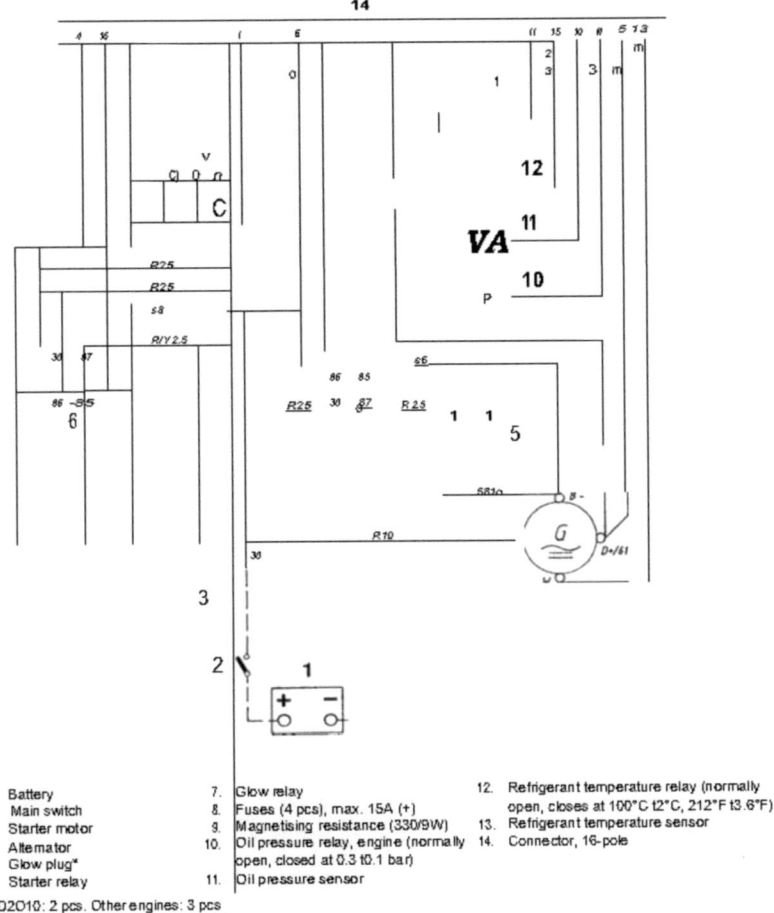

1. Battery
2. Main switch
3. Starter motor
4. Alternator
5. Glow plug*
6. Starter relay
7. Glow relay
8. Fuses (4 pcs), max. 15A (+)
9. Magnetising resistance (330/9W)
10. Oil pressure relay, engine (normally open, closed at 0.3 t0.1 bar)
11. Oil pressure sensor
12. Refrigerant temperature relay (normally open, closes at 100°C t2°C, 212°F t3.6°F)
13. Refrigerant temperature sensor
14. Connector, 16-pole

*MD2010: 2 pcs. Other engines: 3 pcs

Cable colours

BL =	Blue	OR	Orange
LBL =	Light blue	R	Red
BN =	Brown	SB	Black
LBN =	Light brown	W	White
GN =	Green	Y	Yellow
GR =	Grey		

Cable areas in mm² are given after the colour code in the wiring diagram.

Areas not given = 1.0 mm².

Dashed cables are not included from Volvo Penta.

Wiring diagram

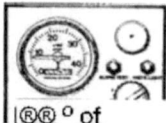

Instrument panel, alternative "B"
MD2010B/C, MD2020B/C, MD2030B/C, MD2040B/C
' (with key switch)

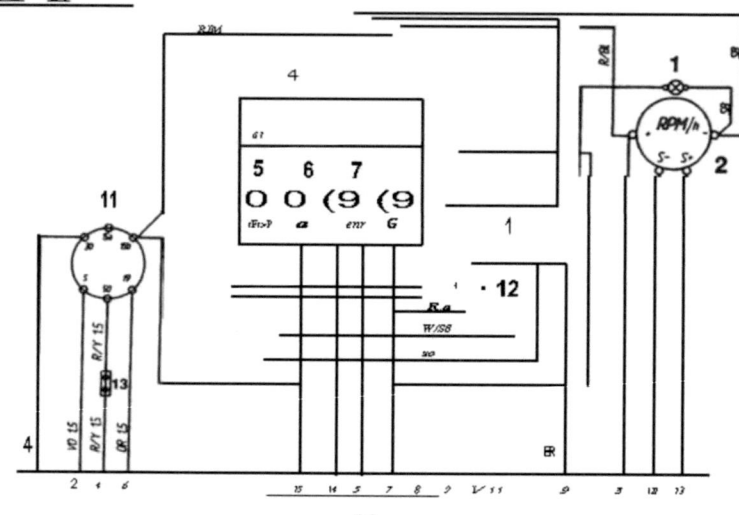

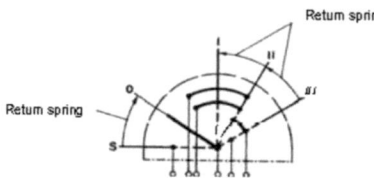

Return spring

1. Instrument lighting
2. Tachometer with built-in hour counter (accessory), alt. blind plug
3. Connector for connection of extra warning display (accessory)
4. Electronics unit (alarm)
5. Warning lamp, refrigerant temperature
6. Warning lamp, oil pressure
7. Warning lamp, charging
8. Control lamp, glowing
9. Switch, instrument lighting
10. Switch - Alarm test/Acknowledging
11. Key switch
12. Alarm
13. Connector for connection of neutral position switch (accessory)
14. 16-pole connection

Cable colours

BL	Blue
BN	Brown
GN	Green
GR	Grey
OR	Orange
R	Red
SB	Black
VO	Violet
W	White
Y	Yellow

Cable areas in mm² are given after the colour code in the wiring diagram.
Areas not given = 1.0 mm²

Wiring diagram

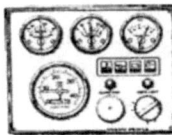

Instrument panel, alternative "C"
MD2010A, MD2020A, MD2030A, MD2040A

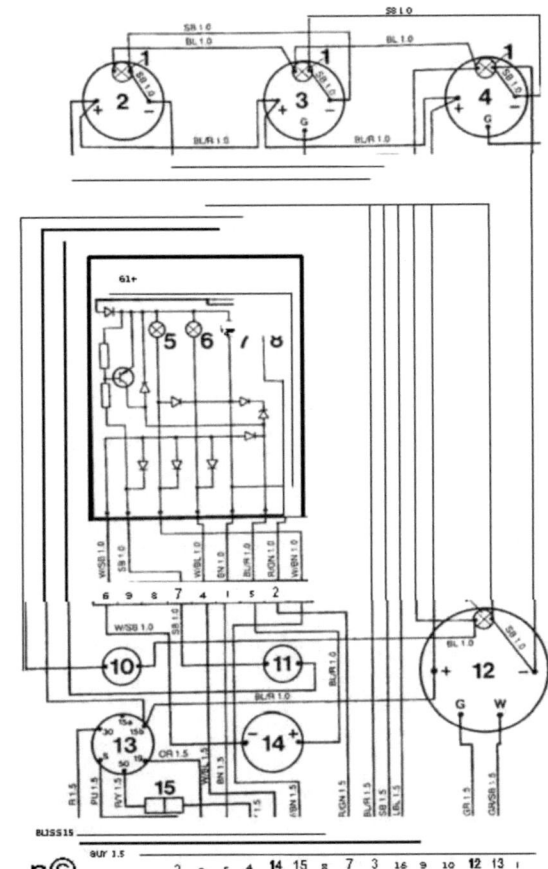

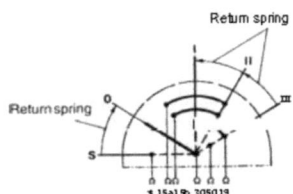

1. Instrument lighting
2. Voltmeter
3. Oil pressure gauge
4. Refrigerant temperature gauge
5. Warning lamp, refrigerant temperature
6. Warning lamp, oil pressure
7. Warning lamp, charging
8. Control lamp, glowing
9. Electronics unit, alarm
10. Switch, instrument lighting
11. Switch - alarm test
12. Tachometer
13. Key switch
14. Alarm
15. Connector for connection of neutral position switch (accessory)
16. 2-pole connection (for extra panel)
17. 16-pole connection

Cable colours

BL	–	Blue
BN	–	Brown
GN	=	Green
GR	–	Grey
OR	–	Orange
R	–	Red
SB	–	Black
VO	–	Violet
W	–	White
Y	–	Yellow

85

Wiring diagram

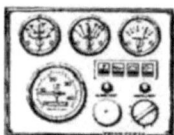

Instrument panel, alternative "C"
MD2010B/C, MD2020B/C, MD2030B/C, MD2040B/C

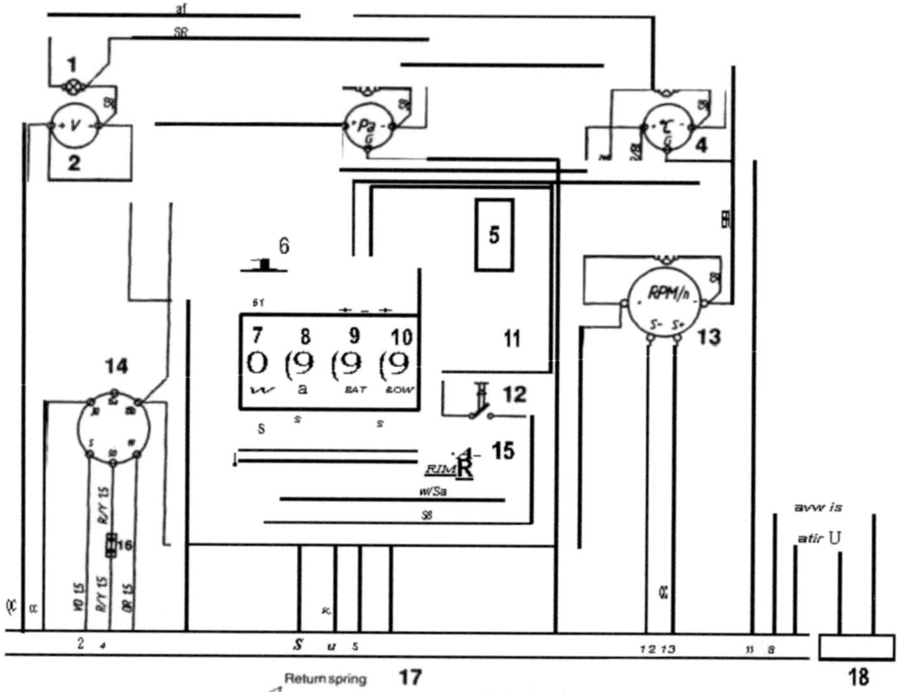

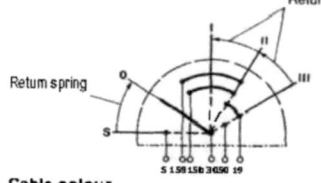

Return spring

Cable colour

BL		Blue
LBL	.	Light blue
BN		Brown
LBN		Light brown
GN	.	Green
GR	.	Grey
OR	.	Orange
R	.	Red
SB	.	Black
VO		Violet
W	.	White
Y	.	Yellow

1. Instrument lighting
2. Voltmeter
3. Oil pressure gauge
4. Refrigerant temperature gauge
5. Connector for connection of extra warning display (accessory)
6. Electronics unit (alarm)
7. Warning lamp, refrigerant temperature
8. Warning lamp, oil pressure
9. Warning lamp, charging
10. Control lamp, glowing
11. Switch, instrument lighting
12. Switch - alarm test/Acknowledging
13. Tachometer with built-in hour counter (accessory), alt. blind plug
14. Key switch
15. Alarm
16. Connector for connection of neutral position switch (accessory)
17. 16-pole connection
18. 2-pole connection (for extra panel)

Cable areas in mm^2 are given after the colour code in the wiring diagram.
Areas not given = 1.0 mm^2

Extra equipment (accessories)

General

Extra equipment which is driven with V-belt*,s via the engine's crankshaft result in an increased load on the crankshaft. It is therefore important that the axial position of the pulley on the crankshaft and the positioning of the equipment in relation to the crankshaft are adjusted to the power takeout of the extra equipment.

The following diagram shows the permissible power takeout at a certain positioning of the pulley and extra equipment.

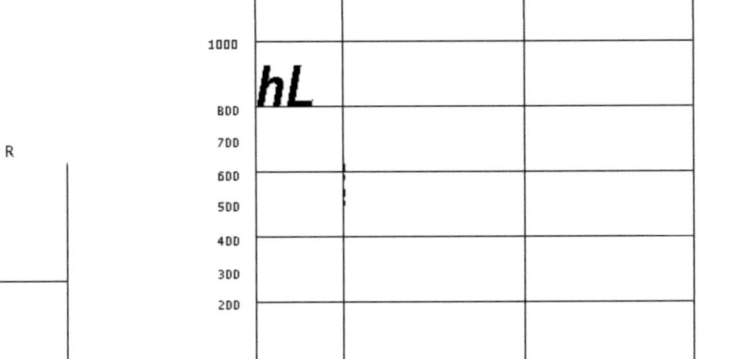

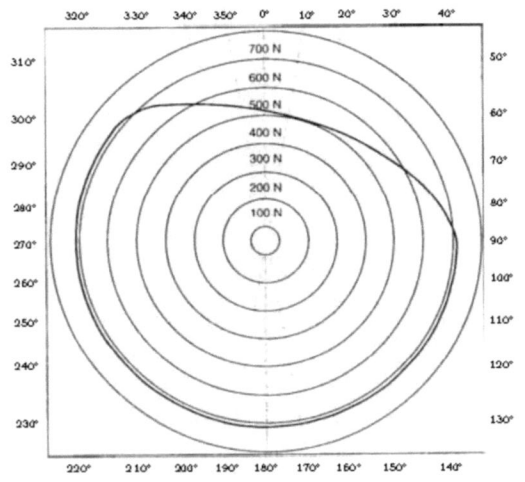

Fig. 127. MD 2010.